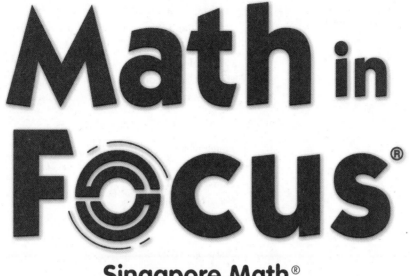

# Math in Focus®

Singapore Math®
by Marshall Cavendish

# Extra Practice
# and Homework

**Program Consultant**
Dr. Fong Ho Kheong

**Authors**
Chelvi Ramakrishnan
Michelle Choo

**Marshall Cavendish**
Education

**U.S. Distributor**

**Houghton Mifflin Harcourt.**
The Learning Company™

Grade
**1A**

© 2020 Marshall Cavendish Education Pte Ltd

**Published by Marshall Cavendish Education**
Times Centre, 1 New Industrial Road, Singapore 536196
Customer Service Hotline: (65) 6213 9688
US Office Tel: (1-914) 332 8888 | Fax: (1-914) 332 8882
E-mail: cs@mceducation.com
Website: www.mceducation.com

Distributed by
**Houghton Mifflin Harcourt**
125 High Street
Boston, MA 02110
Tel: 617-351-5000
Website: www.hmhco.com/programs/math-in-focus

First published 2020

ISBN 978-0-358-10298-4

Printed in China

2 3 4 5 6 7 8          1401          25 24 23 22 21 20
4500799756                            B C D E F

The cover image shows a koala.
Koalas have soft, grey fur and a creamy-colored chest.
They can only be found in some parts of Australia.
Koalas live on eucalyptus trees and eat the leaves.
Koalas are not bears but marsupials.
Marsupials are animals that carry their young around safely inside a pouch.

# Contents

# Preface

Welcome!

**Math** in **FOCUS**® *Extra Practice and Homework* is written to be used with the **Math** in **FOCUS**® *Student Edition*, to support your learning.

This book provides activities and problems that are written to closely follow what you have learned in the Student Edition.

- In **Activities**, you practice what you learned in the Student Edition, to help you master the concepts and build your confidence.

- In **MATH JOURNAL**, you share your thinking, to help you reflect on your learning.

- In **PUT ON YOUR THINKING CAP!**, you challenge yourself to apply what you have learned, as you solve the problems.

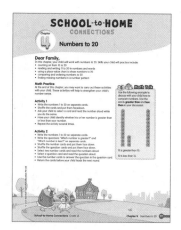

This book also includes **SCHOOL-to-HOME CONNECTIONS**. Each family letter summarizes the learning objectives and the key mathematical vocabulary you are using. The letter also includes one or more activities that your family can do with you to support your learning further.

# SCHOOL-to-HOME
## CONNECTIONS

**Chapter 1**

## Numbers to 10

## Dear Family,

In this chapter, your child will learn numbers to 10. Skills your child will practice include:
- counting to 10
- comparing numbers
- making number patterns

## Math Practice

At the end of this chapter, you may want to carry out these activities with your child. These activities will help to strengthen your child's number sense.

## Activity 1

- Gather 20 plastic beads or cereal hoops, 2 pipe cleaners, and 2 plastic cups.
- Put 10 plastic beads or cereal hoops in each cup.
- Ask your child to thread 0 to 10 beads or cereal hoops onto a pipe cleaner while you do the same, without looking at each other's work.
- Reveal your work to each other when both of you have completed your work.
- Ask your child to count to identify which pipe cleaner has fewer or more objects, or whether both pipe cleaners have the same number of objects.
- Return the objects before playing again.

## Activity 2

- Write the numbers 1 to 10 on separate note cards. Shuffle the cards and put them facedown.
- Have your child select a card and read the number aloud.
- Ask your child to use his or her fingers to show the number.
- Repeat the activity several times.

### Math Talk

When your child **compares** the number of objects in 2 **sets** of objects, he or she identifies whether one set has **fewer** than, **more** than, or the **same** number of objects as the other set. Discuss the following example with your child, helping your child see that each set has the **same** number of objects.

When your child compares 2 numbers, he or she determines if one number is **greater than** or **less than** the other number. Discuss the following example with your child, reading the words aloud.

3 is greater than 2.

2 is less than 3.

BLANK

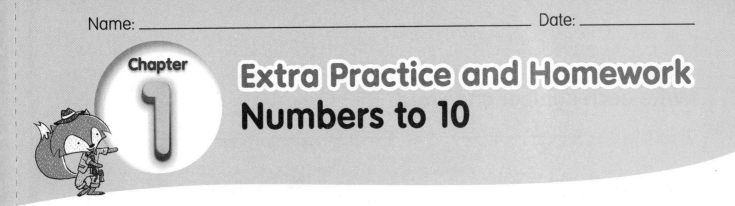

**Chapter 1**

# Extra Practice and Homework
# Numbers to 10

## Activity 1   Counting to 10

**How many are there?**
**Count.**
**Write each number.**

1

4 _____

1 _____

2

8 _____

6 _____

3

6 _____

1 _____

# Count.
# Write each number and word.

**Example**

Number _____ **2** _____

Word _____ **two** _____

---

④ Number _____ 6 _____

Word ___ six ___

---

⑤ Number _____ 8 _____

Word eight

---

⑥ Number _____ 3 _____

Word three

---

⑦ Number _____ 9 _____

Word nine

**8**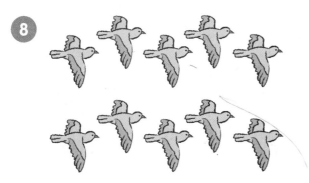

Number ___10___

Word ___ten___

**9**

Number ___1___

Word ___one___

**10**

Number ___7___

Word ___seven___

**11**

Number ___4___

Word ___four___

**12**

Number ___5___

Word ___five___

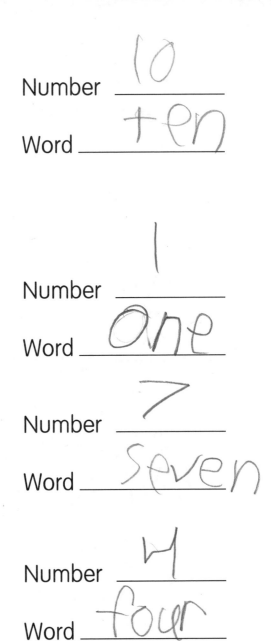

# Count.
# Write each number as a word.

**13**

5 _____

3 _____

8 _____

7 _____

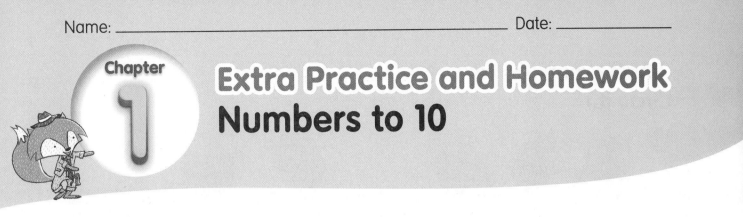

# Chapter 1 — Extra Practice and Homework
## Numbers to 10

## Activity 2 Comparing Numbers

**Which group has more?**
**Circle it.**

**1**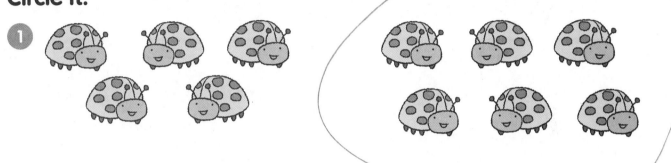

**2**

**3**

# Which group has fewer? Circle it.

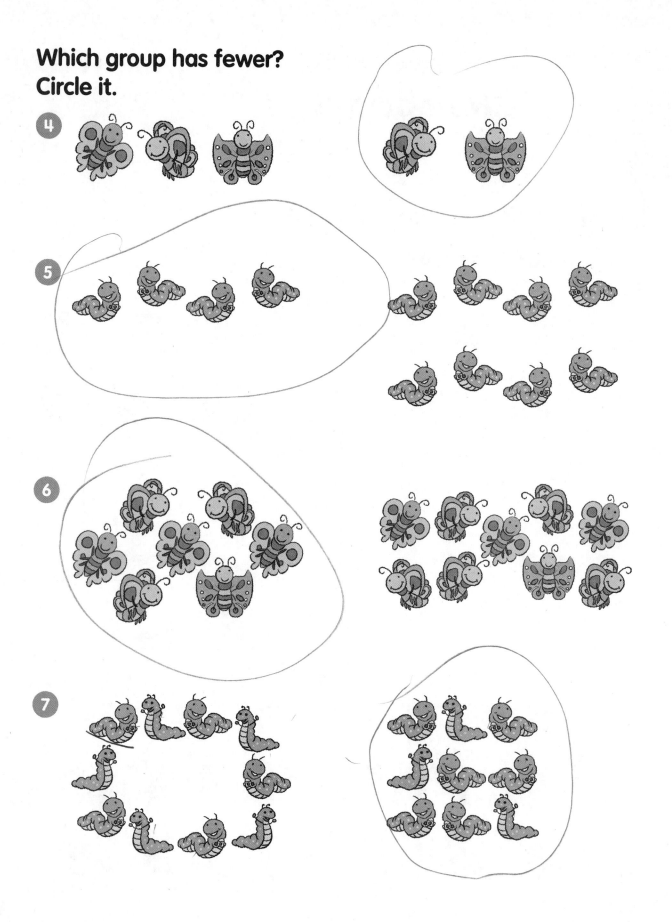

**4**

**5**

**6**

**7**

# Which groups show the same number?
## Circle them.

⑧

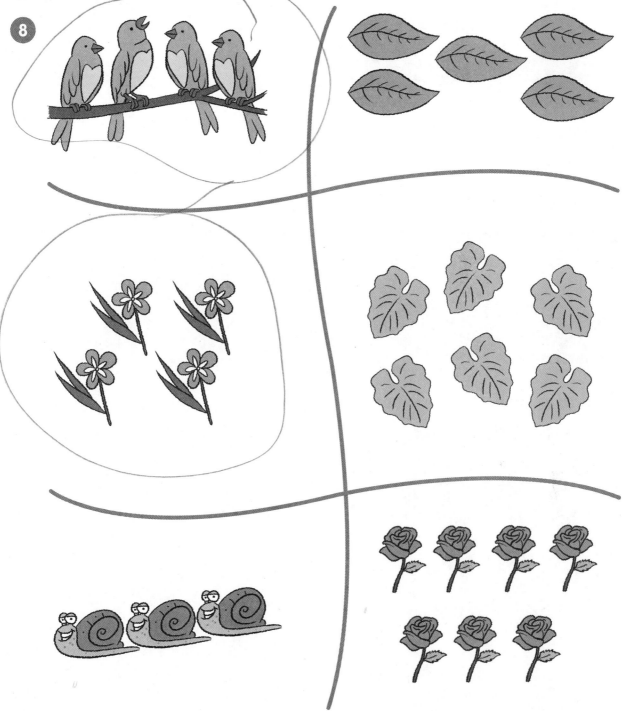

# Which number is greater?
# Write it on the blank.

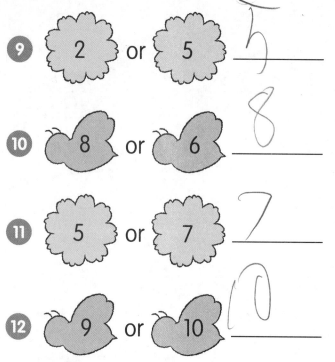

9. 2 or 5    __5__

10. 8 or 6    __8__

11. 5 or 7    __7__

12. 9 or 10    __10__

# Which number is less?
# Write it on the blank.

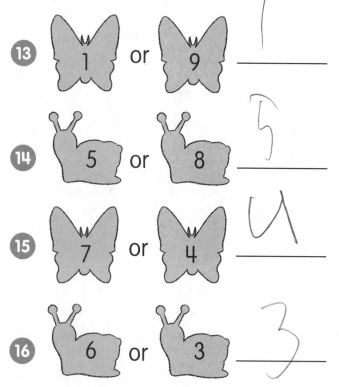

13. 1 or 9    __1__

14. 5 or 8    __5__

15. 7 or 4    __4__

16. 6 or 3    __3__

**Chapter 1**

# Extra Practice and Homework
# Numbers to 10

## Activity 3   Number Patterns

**Fill in each blank.**

1  What is 1 more than 9?

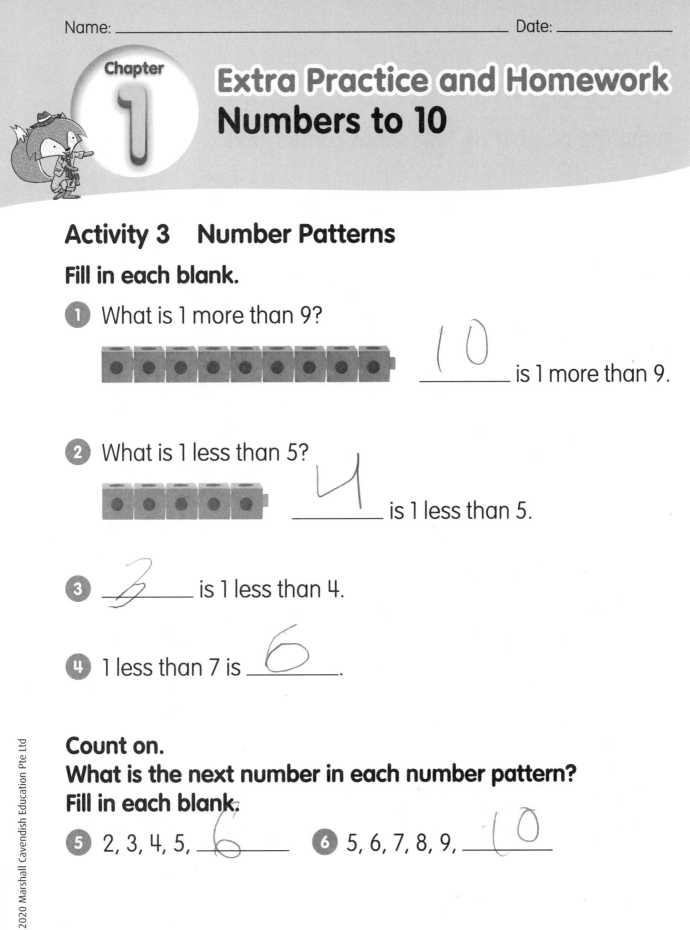

_10_ is 1 more than 9.

2  What is 1 less than 5?

_4_ is 1 less than 5.

3  _3_ is 1 less than 4.

4  1 less than 7 is _6_.

**Count on.**
**What is the next number in each number pattern?**
**Fill in each blank.**

5  2, 3, 4, 5, _6_

6  5, 6, 7, 8, 9, _10_

The 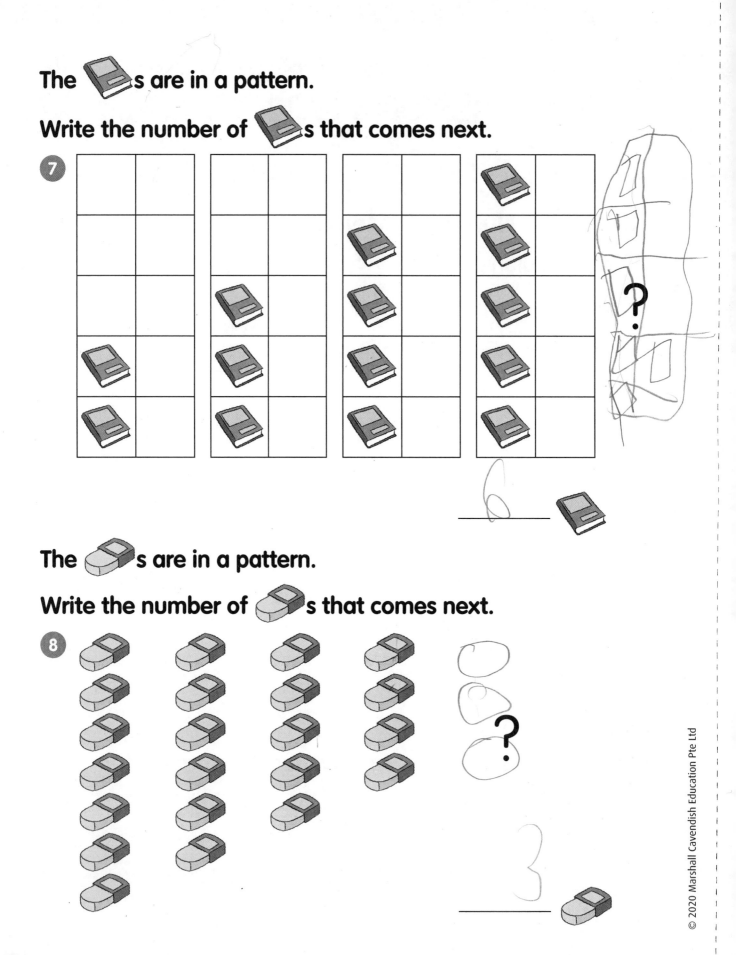s are in a pattern.

Write the number of s that comes next.

7

_____

The s are in a pattern.

Write the number of s that comes next.

8

_____

**Extra Practice and Homework** Grade 1A

© 2020 Marshall Cavendish Education Pte Ltd

**The** 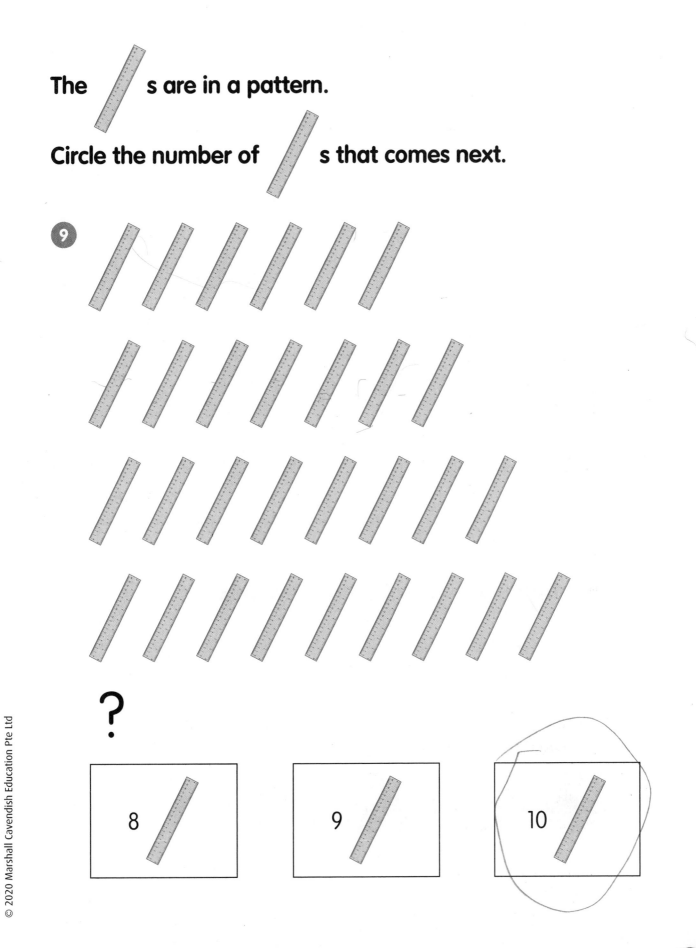 **s are in a pattern.**

**Circle the number of / s that comes next.**

**9**

?

| 8 / | 9 / | 10 / |

# Write the missing number in each number pattern.

**10** 2   3   4   5   6

**11** 4   5   6   7   8

**12** 9   8   7   6   5

**13** 10   9   8   7   6

# Count on from 1 to 10 and fill in each blank.

**14**

1   2   3   4   5

6   7   8   9   10

## Mathematical Habit 3 Construct viable arguments

Look at the given numbers.

0     2     3     5     9

Is there a pattern?
Why?
Write or draw to show why.

no

**1** | **Mathematical Habit** **2** **Use mathematical reasoning**

Daniel is hiding behind a tree.
Which tree is he hiding behind?
Read the clues to find out.
Then, fill in the blank.

> Clues:
> The number on the tree is greater than 2.
> The number on the tree is less than 4.

Daniel is hiding behind tree number _3_.

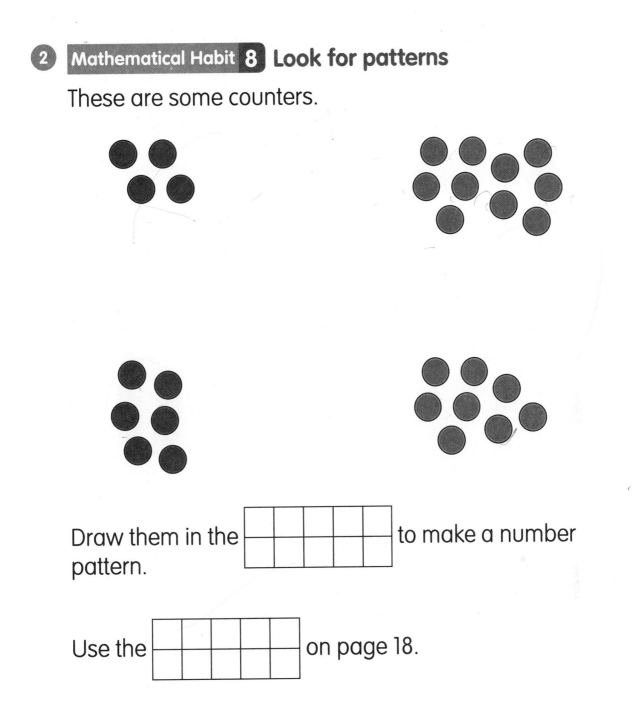

**2** **Mathematical Habit** **8** **Look for patterns**

These are some counters.

Draw them in the ☐☐☐☐☐ to make a number pattern.

Use the ☐☐☐☐☐ on page 18.

PUT ON YOUR THINKING CAP!

# SCHOOL-to-HOME
## CONNECTIONS

**Chapter 2**

# Addition and Subtraction Within 10

## Dear Family,

In this chapter, your child will add and subtract within 10. Skills your child will practice include:

- adding by counting on
- adding using number bonds
- subtracting by counting back and counting on
- subtracting using number bonds
- writing addition and subtraction sentences
- making addition and subtraction stories
- solving real-world problems involving addition and subtraction
- writing fact families
- determining if number sentences are true or false

## Math Practice

At the end of this chapter, you may want to carry out these activities with your child. These activities will help to strengthen your child's understanding of addition and subtraction within 10. Take turns playing. Lead the first round to show your child how to play.

## Activity 1

- Gather a paper plate, a number cube, and 10 identical objects, such as dried beans, macaroni shells, or buttons.
- Put up to 4 objects on the plate and count aloud as you do so.
- Roll the number cube and put the corresponding number of objects on the plate, counting on to find the total number of objects.
- Empty the plate and let your child lead the next round.

## Activity 2

- Gather a paper plate, a number cube, and 10 identical objects, such as dried beans, macaroni shells, or buttons.
- Put 10 objects on the plate and count aloud as you do so.
- Roll the number cube and remove the corresponding number of objects on the plate, counting back to find the number of objects that remain.
- Empty the plate and let your child lead the next round.

### Math Talk

A **number bond** is a visual model of the relationship between a **whole** number and its **parts**. For example, the parts 2 and 3 form a number bond for 5. Discuss the following number bond with your child, encouraging him or her to use the words whole and part in the discussion. Use identical objects such as blocks to support your discussion.

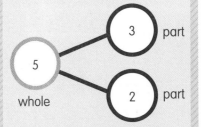

Gather 10 identical objects such as dried beans, and a piece of paper. Draw an **addition** symbol (+) in the middle of the paper. Turn the paper over and draw a **subtraction** symbol (−). Use the objects and both sides of the paper to discuss how to model and solve addition and subtraction problems.

**BLANK**

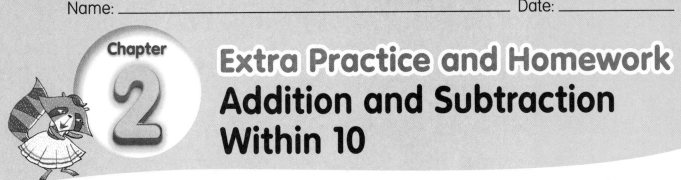

**Chapter 2**

## Extra Practice and Homework
## Addition and Subtraction Within 10

## Activity 1   Making Number Bonds

**Look at each picture.**
**Then, complete each number bond.**

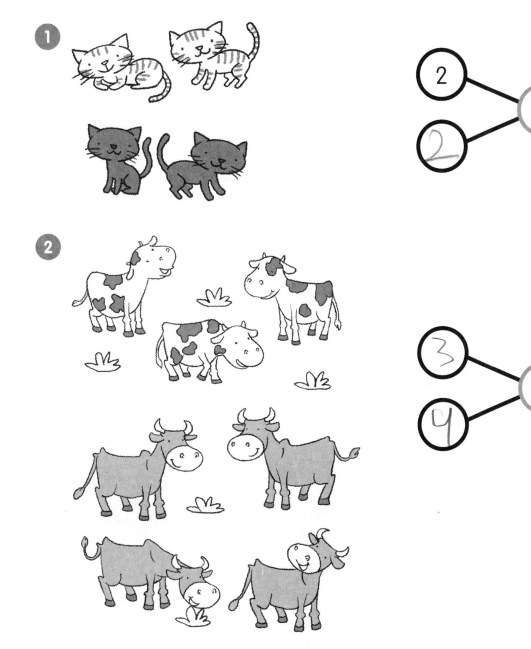

1

2 — 4
2

2

3 — 7
4

# Complete each number bond.

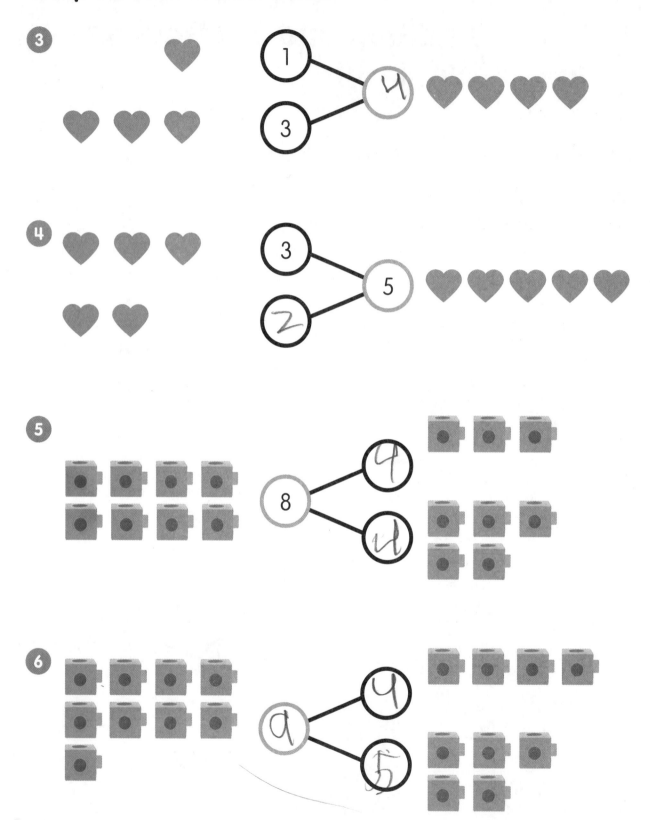

3

$\begin{array}{l} 1 \\ 3 \end{array}$ — 4

4

$\begin{array}{l} 3 \\ 2 \end{array}$ — 5

5

8 — 4 / 4

6

9 — 4 / 5

## Write each missing number.

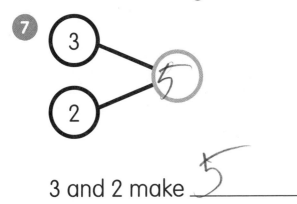

**7**

3 and 2 make _5_.

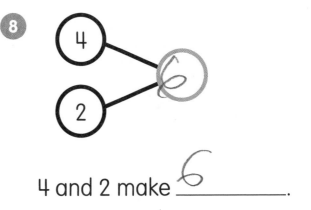

**8**

4 and 2 make _6_.

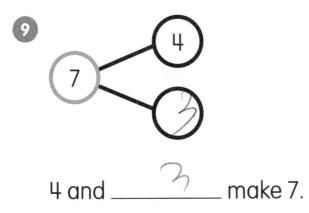

**9**

4 and _3_ make 7.

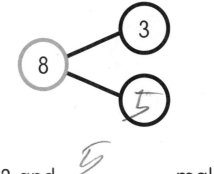

**10**

3 and _5_ make 8.

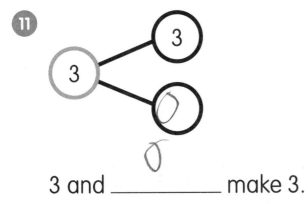

**11**

3 and _0_ make 3.

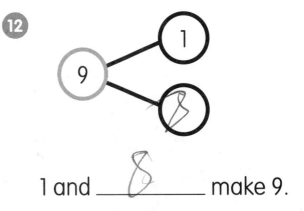

**12**

1 and _8_ make 9.

# Make a number bond for each number.

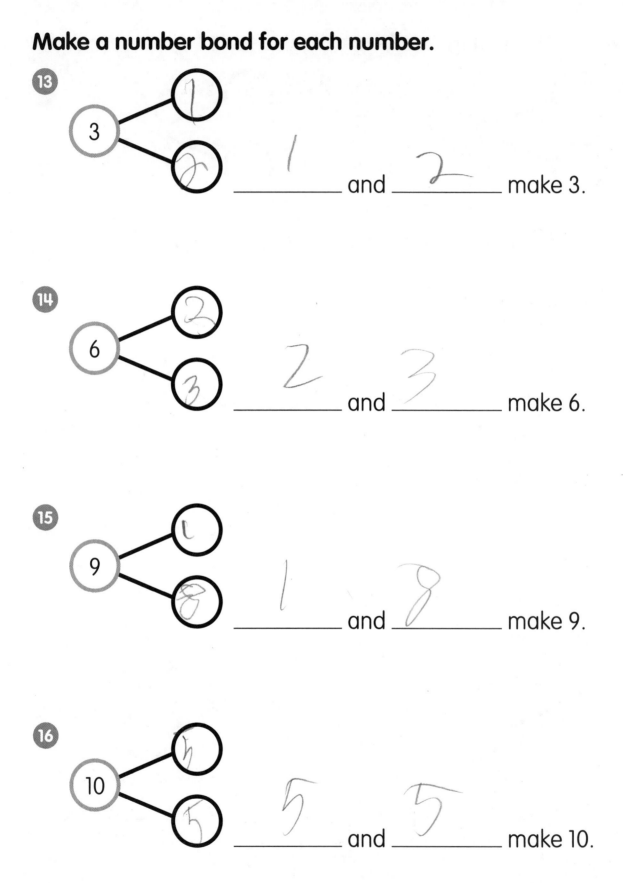

**13**

3 — 1, 2

_____1_____ and _____2_____ make 3.

**14**

6 — 2, 3

_____2_____ and _____3_____ make 6.

**15**

9 — 1, 8

_____1_____ and _____8_____ make 9.

**16**

10 — 5, 5

_____5_____ and _____5_____ make 10.

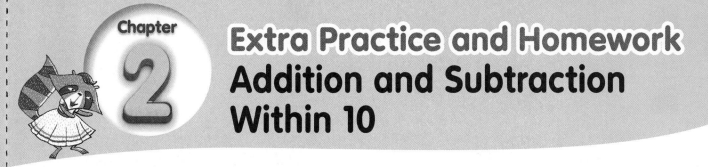

## Activity 2   Ways to Add

**Complete each number bond.**

1

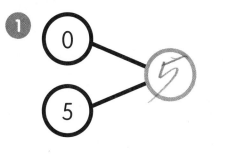

0 / 5 — 5

5 / 0 — 5

2

8 / 2 — 10

2 / 8 — 10

## Add.
## Use number bonds to help you.

3  How many books are there in all?

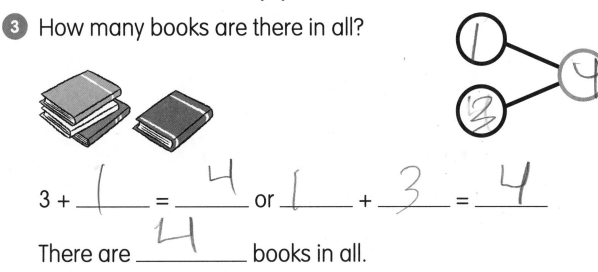

1 / 2 — 4

$3 + \underline{1} = \underline{4}$ or $\underline{1} + \underline{3} = \underline{4}$

There are $\underline{4}$ books in all.

How many rabbits are there in all?

$\underline{5}$ + $\underline{2}$ = $\underline{7}$ or $\underline{2}$ + $\underline{5}$ = $\underline{7}$

There are _____ rabbits in all.

5 How many mice are there in all?

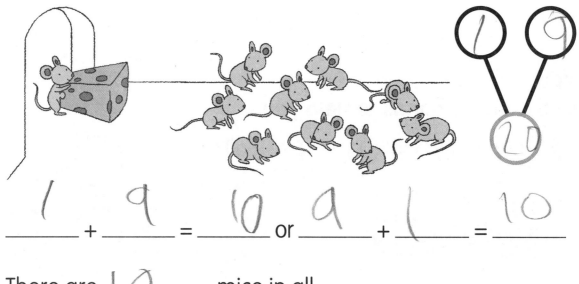

$\underline{1}$ + $\underline{9}$ = $\underline{10}$ or $\underline{9}$ + $\underline{1}$ = $\underline{10}$

There are $\underline{10}$ mice in all.

# Add.
## Count on from the greater number.
## Fill in each missing number.

**6**

| 3 | | | 4 | | 5 |

3 + 2 = _____

**7**

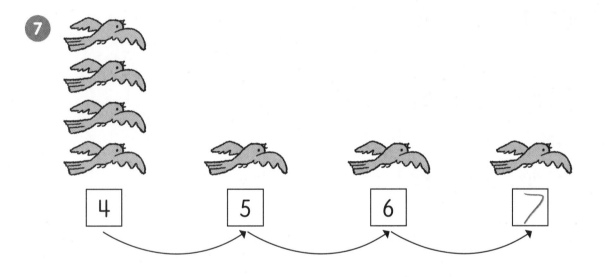

| 4 | 5 | 6 | 7 |

4 + 3 = _____

**8**

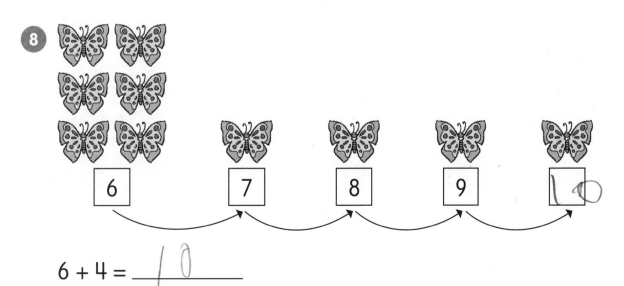

| 6 | 7 | 8 | 9 | 10 |

6 + 4 = ____ 10

## Add.
## Count on from the greater number.

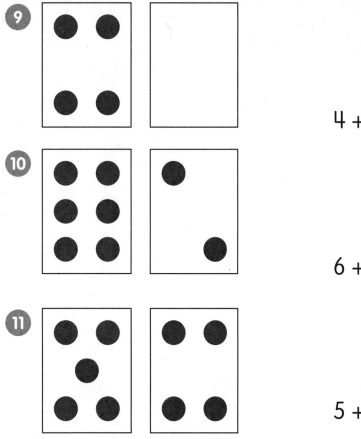

**9** 

$4 + 0 = \underline{4}$

**10** 

$6 + 2 = \underline{8}$

**11** 

$5 + 4 = \underline{9}$

## Add.
## Use the counting tape to help you.

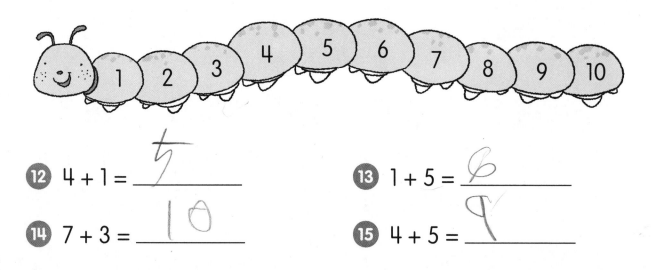

**12** $4 + 1 = \underline{5}$

**13** $1 + 5 = \underline{6}$

**14** $7 + 3 = \underline{10}$

**15** $4 + 5 = \underline{9}$

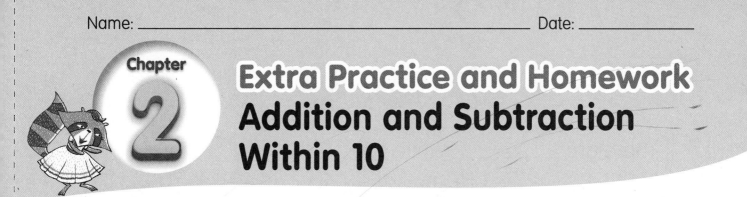

**Chapter 2**

# Extra Practice and Homework
## Addition and Subtraction Within 10

## Activity 3   Making Addition Stories

**Look at each picture.**
**Make an addition story.**
**Then, fill in each blank.**

**1**

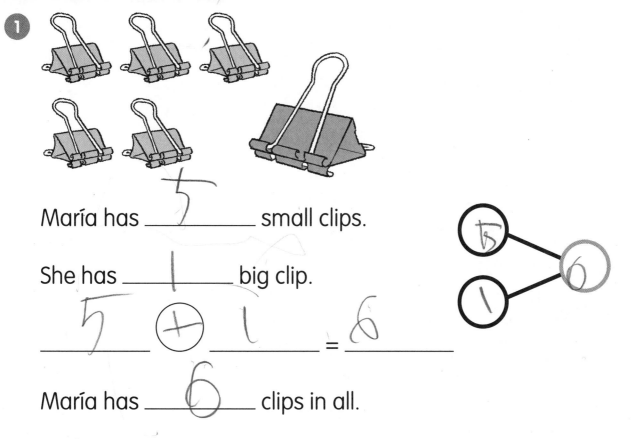

María has ___5___ small clips.

She has ___1___ big clip.

___5___ ⊕ ___1___ = ___6___

María has ___6___ clips in all.

**2**

There are _____2_____ white caps.

There are _____3_____ black caps.

_____2_____ ⊕ _____3_____ = _____5_____

There are _____5_____ caps in all.

**3**

_____ birds are singing.

_____ more birds join them.

_____ ⃝ _____ = _____

There are _____ birds in all.

**4**

There are _____6_____ crayons in the pencil case.

_____2_____ crayons are not in the pencil case.

_____6_____ ⊕ _____2_____ = _____8_____

There are _____8_____ crayons in all.

**5**

There are ___7___ potatoes in a pot.

Mr. Brown puts in ___3___ more potatoes.

___7___ ⊕ ___3___ = ___10___

There are ___10___ potatoes in the pot now.

**6**

Blake

Bella

Blake folds _____5_____ paper flowers.

Bella folds _____5_____ paper flowers.

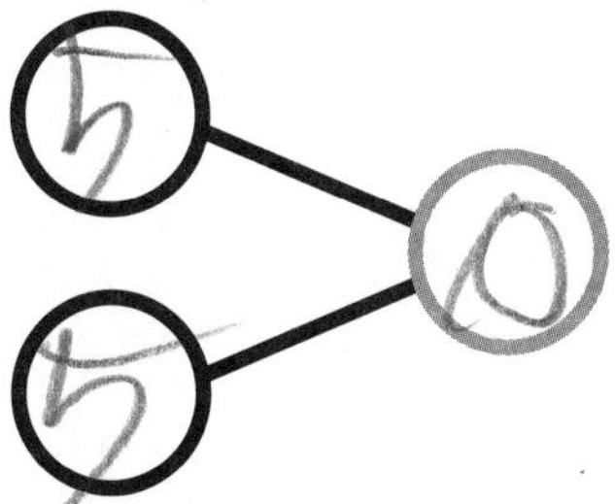

5
5

⑤ — ⓪
⑤

_____5_____ ⊕ _____5_____ = _____10_____
10

They fold _____10_____ paper flowers in all.

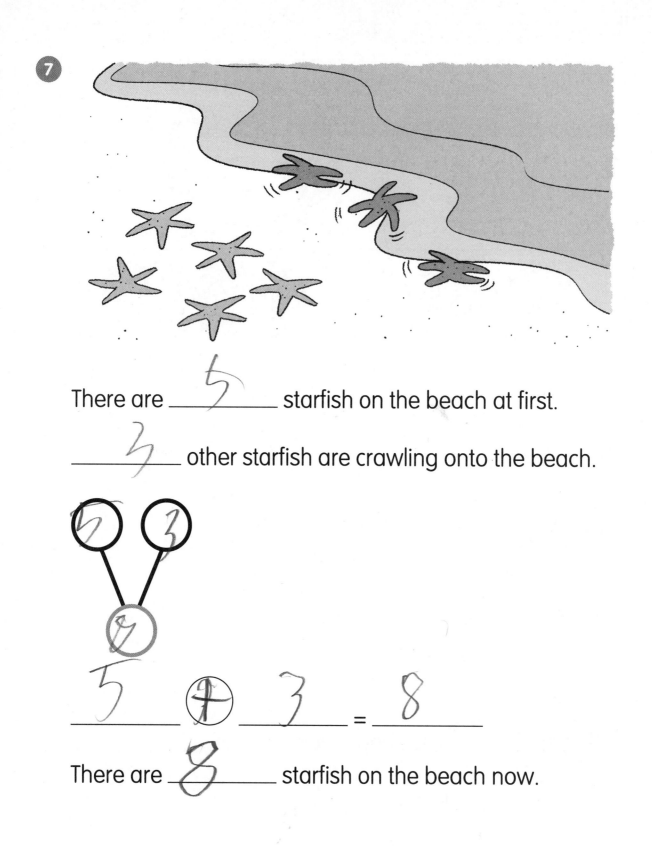

**7**

There are _____5_____ starfish on the beach at first.

_____3_____ other starfish are crawling onto the beach.

_____5_____ ⊕ _____3_____ = _____8_____

There are _____8_____ starfish on the beach now.

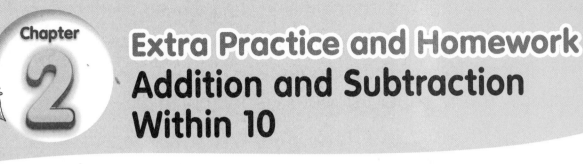

**Chapter 2**

# Extra Practice and Homework
## Addition and Subtraction Within 10

## Activity 4    Real-World Problems: Addition

**Solve.**

1. Matthew has 4 T-shirts.
   He receives 2 T-shirts as presents.
   How many T-shirts does Matthew
   have in all?

$$\underline{\quad 4 \quad} \oplus \underline{\quad 2 \quad} = \underline{\quad 6 \quad}$$

Matthew has ___6___ T-shirts in all.

2. Malia has 7 hairbands.
   Her sister gives her 1 hairband.
   How many hairbands does
   Malia have in all?

> You can use the four-step problem-solving model to help you.

$$\underline{\quad 7 \quad} \oplus \underline{\quad 1 \quad} = \underline{\quad 8 \quad}$$

Malia has ___8___ hairbands in all.

**3** Henry folds 7 paper fish.
He then folds 3 more paper fish.
How many paper fish does Henry fold in all?

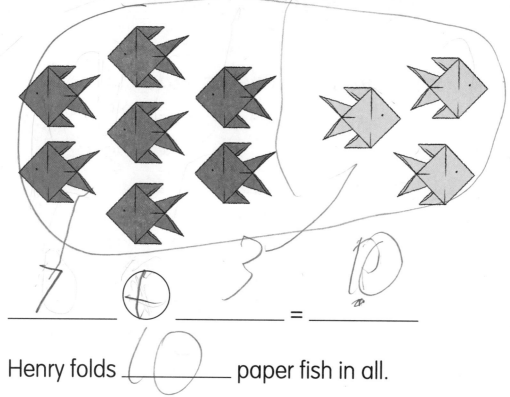

_____  7  (+)  _____  3  =  _____  10

Henry folds ____10____ paper fish in all.

**4** Ms. Black irons 3 dresses on Monday morning.
She irons 4 more dresses in the afternoon.
How many dresses does Ms. Black iron in all?

_____  3  (+)  _____  4  =  _____  7

Ms. Black irons ____7____ dresses in all.

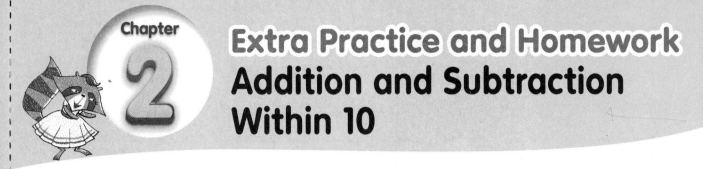

**Chapter 2**

# Extra Practice and Homework
# Addition and Subtraction Within 10

## Activity 5   Ways to Subtract

**Subtract.**
**Count on from the number that is less.**
**Draw arrows to help you.**

**1** How many muffins are left?

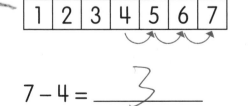

| 1 | 2 | 3 | 4 | 5 | 6 | 7 |

7 − 4 = _____3_____

_____3_____ muffins are left.

2 How many eggs does the man break on falling down?

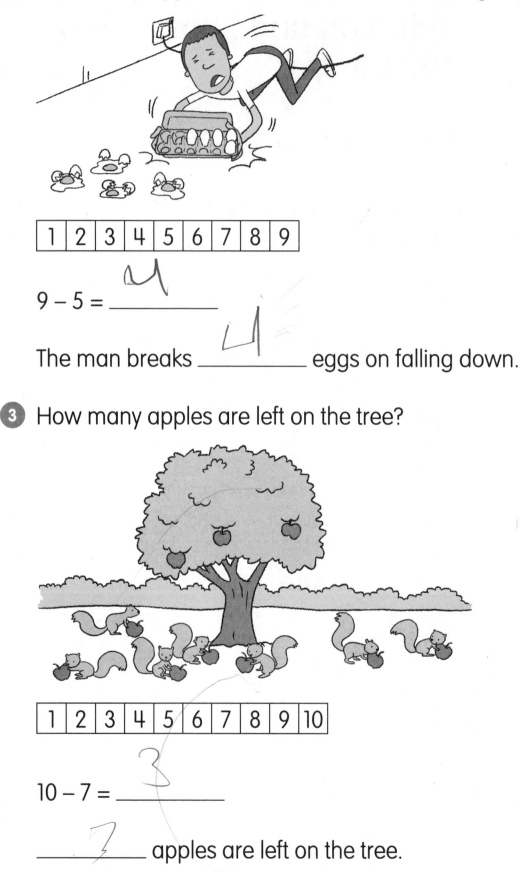

| 1 | 2 | 3 | 4 | 5 | 6 | 7 | 8 | 9 |

$9 - 5 =$ _____ 4

The man breaks _____ 4 eggs on falling down.

3 How many apples are left on the tree?

| 1 | 2 | 3 | 4 | 5 | 6 | 7 | 8 | 9 | 10 |

$10 - 7 =$ _____ 3

_____ 3 apples are left on the tree.

How many chicks are under Mother Hen's wings?

| 1 | 2 | 3 | 4 | 5 | 6 | 7 |

$7 - 4 =$ __3__

__3__ chicks are under Mother Hen's wings.

**btract.**
**unt back from the greater number.**
**w arrows to help you.**

$8 - 3 =$ __5__

| 1 | 2 | 3 | 4 | 5 | 6 | 7 | 8 |

$7 - 2 =$ __5__

| 1 | 2 | 3 | 4 | 5 | 6 | 7 |

$10 - 4 =$ __6__

| 1 | 2 | 3 | 4 | 5 | 6 | 7 | 8 | 9 | 10 |

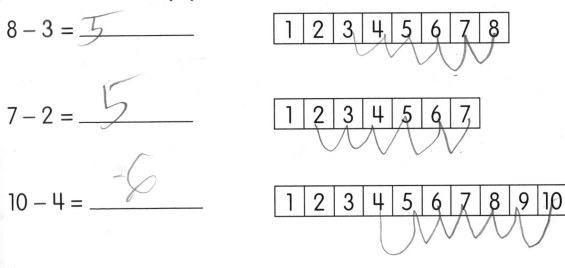

© 2020 Marshall Cavendish Education Pte Ltd

**Subtract.**
**Count on from the number that is less.**
**Draw arrows to help you.**

**4** 9 − 6 = _____

| 1 | 2 | 3 | 4 | 5 | 6 |
|---|---|---|---|---|---|

**5** 8 − 4 = _4___

| 1 | 2 | 3 | 4 | 5 | 6 |
|---|---|---|---|---|---|

**6** 10 − 6 = _____

| 1 | 2 | 3 | 4 | 5 | 6 |
|---|---|---|---|---|---|

**Subtract.**
**Count back from the greater number.**
**Draw arrows to help you.**

**7** How many pails are empty?

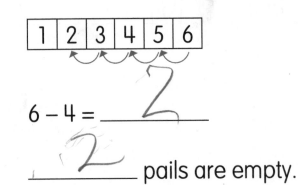

| 1 | 2 | 3 | 4 | 5 | 6 |
|---|---|---|---|---|---|

6 − 4 = __2___

_____2_____ pails are empty.

**Use a number bond to subtract.**
**Then, fill in each blank.**

**12** How many people are left in the line?

$$\underline{\phantom{6}6\phantom{6}} + \underline{\phantom{1}1\phantom{1}} = \underline{\phantom{7}7\phantom{7}}$$

So, $\underline{\phantom{7}7\phantom{7}} - \underline{\phantom{1}1\phantom{1}} = \underline{\phantom{6}6\phantom{6}}$.

$$\underline{\phantom{7}7\phantom{7}} - \underline{\phantom{1}1\phantom{1}} = \underline{\phantom{6}6\phantom{6}}$$

$\underline{\phantom{6}6\phantom{6}}$ people are left in the line.

## Use a number bond to subtract.
## Then, fill in each blank.

**13** 4 − 2 = ?

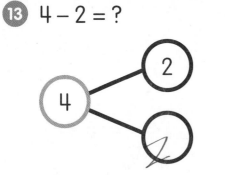

2 + _____2_____ = 4

So, 4 − 2 = _____2_____.

**14** 9 − 3 = ?

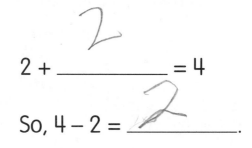

3 + _____6_____ = 9

So, 9 − _____6_____ = _____3_____.

**15** 7 − 6 = ?

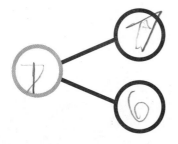

6 + _____1_____ = 7

So, 7 − _____ = _____.

**16** 10 − 6 = ?

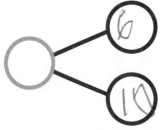

_____ + _____ = 10

So, 10 − _____ = _____.

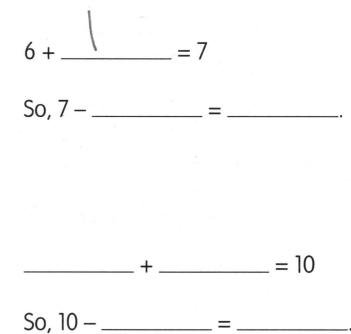
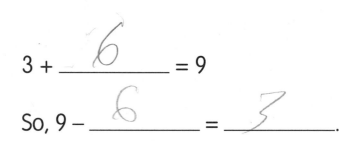

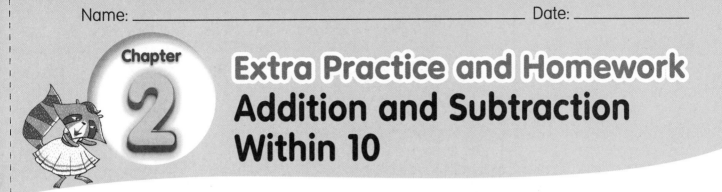

### Chapter 2

## Extra Practice and Homework
## Addition and Subtraction Within 10

## Activity 6   Making Subtraction Stories

Look at each picture.
Make a subtraction story.
Then, fill in each blank.

**1**

Jess bakes 7 cookies.

Her children eat _____2_____ cookies.

_____2_____ (+) _____5_____ = _____7_____
     3

_____3_____ cookies are left.

**2**

There are _8_ stars.

Lucy colors _2_ stars.

_2_ (+) _6_ = _8_

_2_ stars are not colored.

**3**

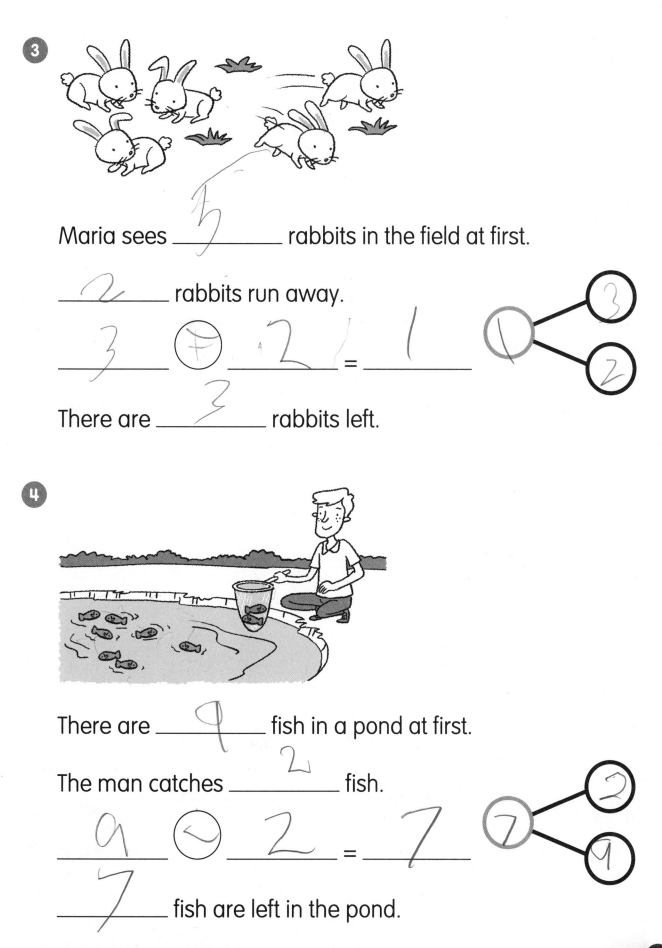

Maria sees _____3_____ rabbits in the field at first.

_____2_____ rabbits run away.

_____3_____ ⊝ _____2_____ = _____1_____

There are _____3_____ rabbits left.

**4**

There are _____9_____ fish in a pond at first.

The man catches _____2_____ fish.

_____9_____ ⊝ _____2_____ = _____7_____

_____7_____ fish are left in the pond.

**5**

There are _____9_____ watering cans in all.

Farmer Carter fills _____1_____ watering cans with water.

_____9_____ ⃝ ____1____ = ____8____

_____4_____ watering cans do not have water.

**6**

Alex has _____10_____ apples and oranges in all.

_____6_____ are apples.

_____10_____ ⃝− ____4____ = ____6____

Alex has _____4_____ oranges.

### Activity 7   Real-World Problems: Subtraction

**Solve.**

1  Ms. Davis has 8 carrots.
She uses 5 of them to bake a carrot cake.
How many carrots are left?

_____ $8$ ◯ $-$ _____ $5$ = _____ $3$   ◯ $8$

_____ $3$ carrots are left.

You can use the four-step problem-solving model to help you.

**2** Mr. Lee has 7 ties.
4 of them have designs on them.
The rest are plain ones.
How many plain ties does Mr. Lee have?

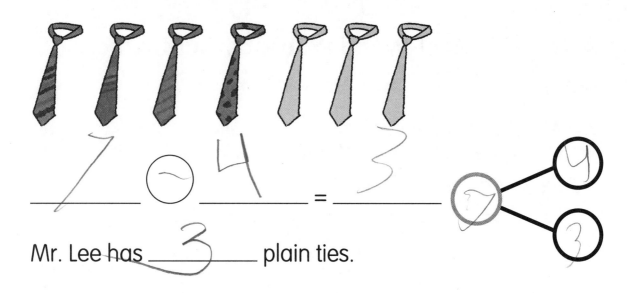

_7_ $\bigcirc-$ _4_ = _3_

Mr. Lee has __3__ plain ties.

**3** There are 8 pears.
Alan and his sister eat 4 of them.
How many pears are left?

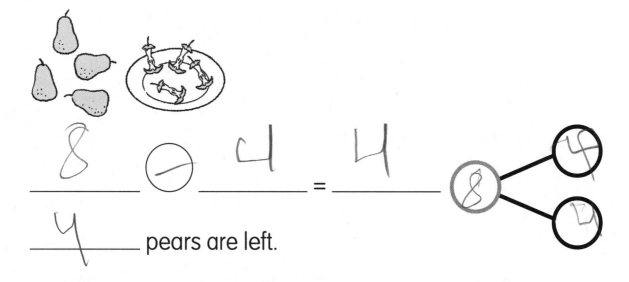

_8_ $\bigcirc-$ _4_ = _4_

__4__ pears are left.

4. There are 10 bracelets at a shop.
A lady buys 7 of them.
How many bracelets are left?

10 ◯− 7 = 3

3 bracelets are left.

5. There are 9 trees in a park.
7 trees are short and the rest are tall.
How many tall trees are there?

9 ◯− 7 =

There are _____ tall trees.

**6** Liam catches 7 shrimps.
He gives 3 shrimps to his sister.
How many shrimps does Liam have left?

7 ⊖ 3 = 4

Liam has ___4___ shrimps left.

7

**7** There are 9 animals on a farm.
3 of them are cows and the rest are sheep.
How many sheep are there?

9 ⊖ 3 = 6

There are ___ sheep.

9

### Chapter 2

# Extra Practice and Homework
## Addition and Subtraction Within 10

## Activity 8   Making Fact Families

Make a fact family for each picture.

1

$$4 + 1 = 5 \qquad 5 - 4 = 1$$
$$1 + 4 = 5 \qquad 5 - 1 = 4$$

2

$$6 + 2 = 8 \qquad 8 - 6 = 2$$
$$2 + 6 = 8 \qquad 8 - 2 = 6$$

**3**

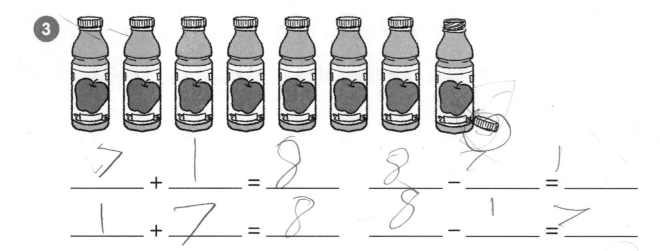

$$\underline{\quad 7 \quad} + \underline{\quad 1 \quad} = \underline{\quad 8 \quad} \qquad \underline{\quad 8 \quad} - \underline{\quad 7 \quad} = \underline{\quad 1 \quad}$$

$$\underline{\quad 1 \quad} + \underline{\quad 7 \quad} = \underline{\quad 8 \quad} \qquad \underline{\quad 8 \quad} - \underline{\quad 1 \quad} = \underline{\quad 7 \quad}$$

## Fill in each blank.
## Use related facts to help you.

**4** Silas buys some notebooks.
He uses 3 notebooks.
4 notebooks are not used.
How many notebooks does
Silas buy?

$$\underline{\quad 7 \quad} - 3 = 4$$

$3 + 4 = \underline{\quad 7 \quad}$ is the related addition fact.

So, $\underline{\quad 7 \quad} - 3 = 4$.

Silas buys $\underline{\quad 7 \quad}$ notebooks.

**5** Brooke and her brother have 10 peaches.
They eat some peaches.
They have 8 peaches now.
How many peaches do Brooke and her brother eat?

$8 +$ _____?_____ $= 10$

$10 - 8 =$ ___2___ is the related subtraction fact.

So, $8 +$ ___2___ $= 10$.

Brooke and her brother eat ___2___ peaches.

**Fill in each blank.**
**Use related facts to help you.**

**6** ___5___ $- 2 = 3$

**7** ___9___ $- 7 = 2$

**8** $10 -$ ___4___ $= 6$

**9** $4 +$ ___5___ $= 9$

$2 + 3 =$ ___5___

So, ___5___ $- 2 = 3$.

**Fill in each blank.**

**10** Is 9 − 7 = 3̲ a true number sentence?

9 − 7 = _____2_____

Is _____2_____ the same as 3? _____NO_____ (No̸ / Yes)

So, this number sentence is _____false_____. (true / false̸)

**Color the objects with a number sentence that is true.**

**11**

| 4 + 4 = 8 | 5 − 0 = 4 | 9 − 6 = 3 |

**12**

8 − 2 = 3

4 + 3 = 6

7 + 0 = 0 + 7

6 + 1 = 10 − 3

## Mathematical Habit 4 Use mathematical models

Fill in each blank with a number.

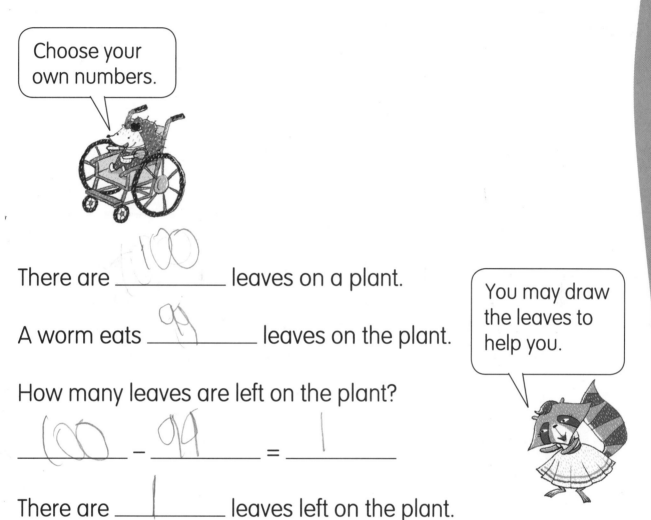

Choose your own numbers.

There are ___100___ leaves on a plant.

A worm eats ___99___ leaves on the plant.

You may draw the leaves to help you.

How many leaves are left on the plant?

___100___ – ___99___ = ___1___

There are ___1___ leaves left on the plant.

**1** | Mathematical Habit **1** | **Persevere in solving problems**

Make two addition sentences that are true.
Use each number once only.

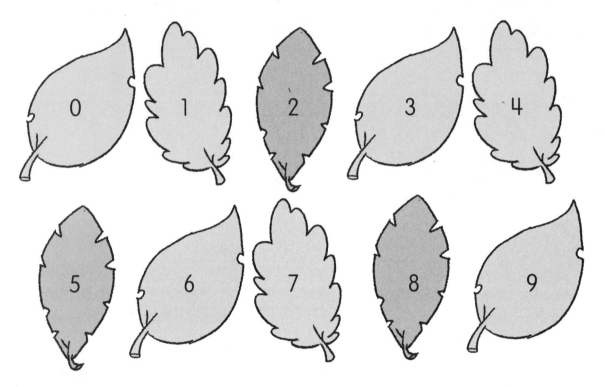

Write your addition sentences on the next page.
Use the number bonds to help you.

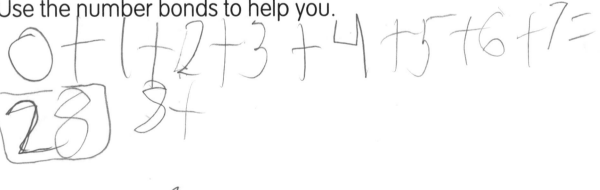

0 + 1 + 2 + 3 + 4 + 5 + 6 + 7 =

28  8 +

8 + 9 = 17

$\underline{\quad 3 \quad} + \underline{\quad 3 \quad} + \underline{\quad 4 \quad} = 10$

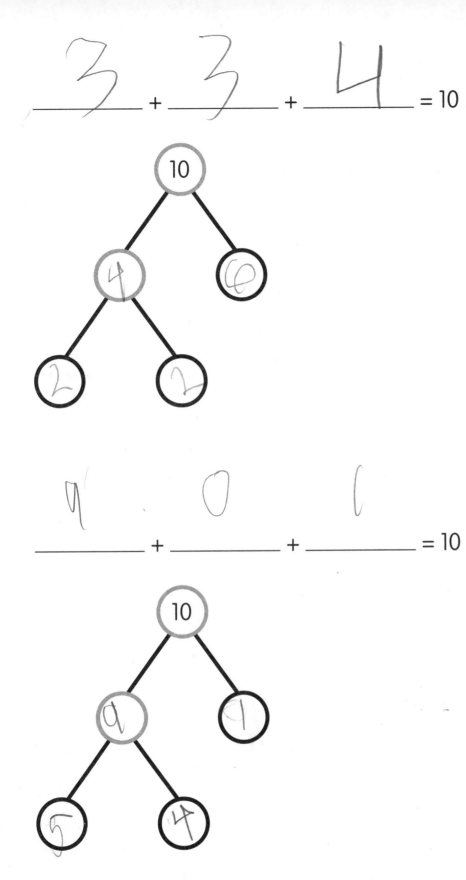

$\underline{\quad 9 \quad} + \underline{\quad 0 \quad} + \underline{\quad 1 \quad} = 10$

**2** **Mathematical Habit 1** **Persevere in solving problems**

Ellie thinks of two numbers.
She gives Max clues and asks him to guess the numbers.

Clues:
When she adds them, she gets 8.
When she subtracts one from the other, she gets 2.

What are the two numbers?

$5 + 3$

1  7
2  6
3  5
4 - 4 = 0
⑤ - 3 = 2
6  2
7  1

# SCHOOL-to-HOME CONNECTIONS

## Shapes and Patterns

## Dear Family,

In this chapter, your child will explore flat and solid shapes. Skills your child will practice include:
- identifying, classifying, and describing flat shapes
- identifying, classifying, and sorting solid shapes
- composing new shapes and models
- using shapes to identify, extend, and create patterns

### Math Practice

At the end of this chapter, you may want to carry out these activities with your child. These activities will help to strengthen your child's understanding of flat and solid shapes.

### Activity 1

- Look for examples of rectangular prisms, cubes, and cylinders in your food cupboard. Sort the objects by their shapes.

### Activity 2

- Visit a library and read books about shapes, such as *Shapes, Shapes, Shapes* by Tana Hoban; *Shapes That Roll* by Karen Nagel; *Bees, Snails, & Peacock Tails: Patterns & Shapes . . . Naturally* by Betsy Franco; and *Shape by Shape* by Suse MacDonald.

### Activity 3

- Encourage your child to draw his or her favorite animal using circles, squares, triangles, and rectangles. Then, challenge your child to create the same animal using solid shapes. Use store-bought or homemade clay or dough to make spheres, cubes, pyramids, and rectangular prisms.

### Math Talk

Examine a piece of paper together. Count the paper's **sides** and **corners**. If the paper's sides are all equal, it is a square. If the opposite sides are equal, it is a rectangle.

Next, look at a cereal box. Count the sides and corners. Identify the box as a **rectangular prism**, which is a type of solid shape.

SCHOOL TO HOME

**BLANK**

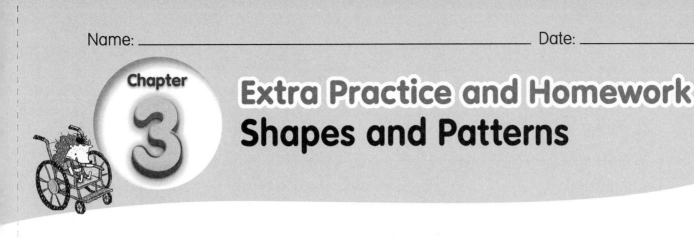

## Activity 1  Exploring Flat Shapes

Trace each shape.
Then, match each shape to its name.

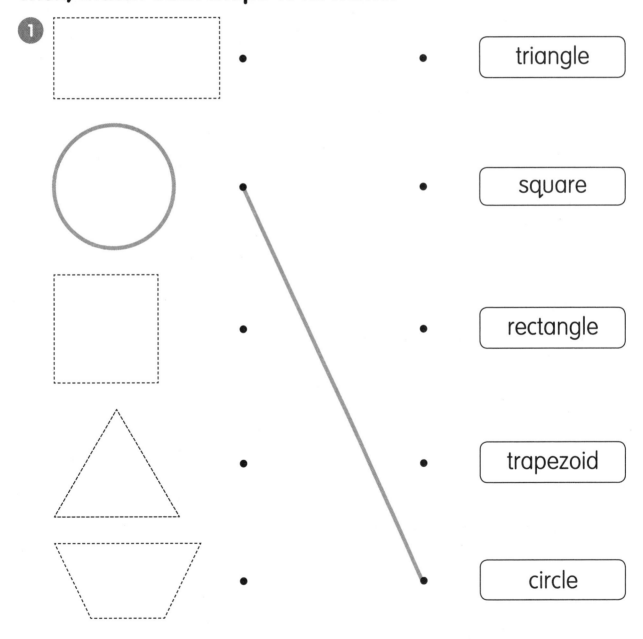

# Color the shapes.

**2** Squares

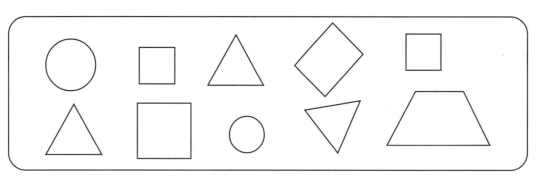

**3** Triangles

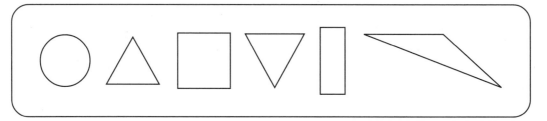

**4** Rectangles

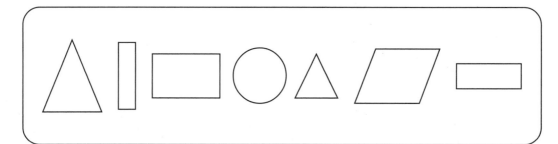

**5** The shapes that are not circles

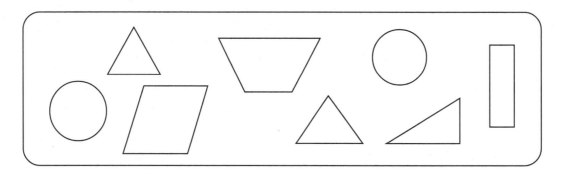

**Which shape is "not" in each set?**
**Circle the correct answer.**

**6** Set A

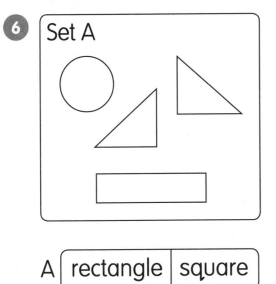

A | rectangle | square |
is not in this set.

**7** Set B

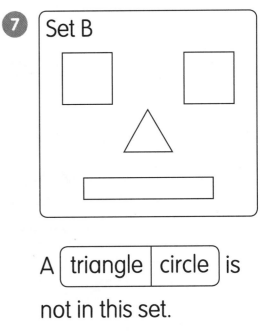

A | triangle | circle | is
not in this set.

**Look at the shapes.**
**Sort and count each shape.**
**Then, fill in each table.**

**8**

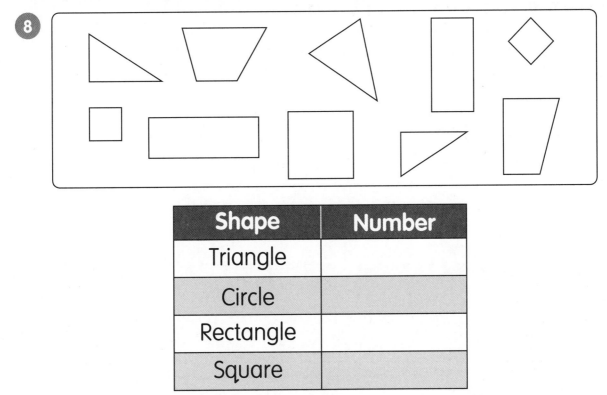

| Shape | Number |
|---|---|
| Triangle | |
| Circle | |
| Rectangle | |
| Square | |

**9**

| Shape | Number |
|---|---|
| Triangle | |
| Circle | |
| Rectangle | |
| Trapezoid | |

## How are the shapes grouped?
## Write the correct letter in the blank.

**10**

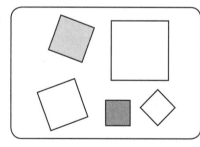  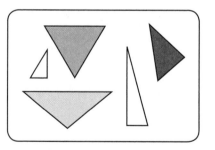

a  By color     b  By shape     c  By size     _____

## Sort the shapes.
## Then, fill in each table with the letter on each shape.

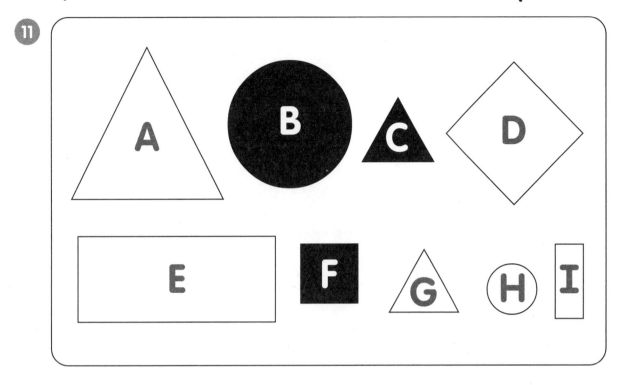

Shape

| Circle | Triangle | Square | Rectangle |
|--------|----------|--------|-----------|
|        |          |        |           |

Size

| Big | Small |
|-----|-------|
|     |       |

Color

| Black | White |
|-------|-------|
|       |       |

**Do the shapes show halves?**
**Write "Yes" or "No" in each blank.**

12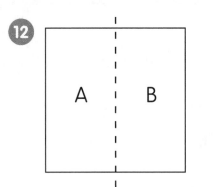

Shapes A and B _____

13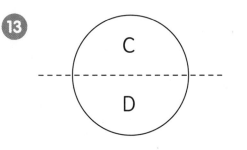

Shapes C and D _____

14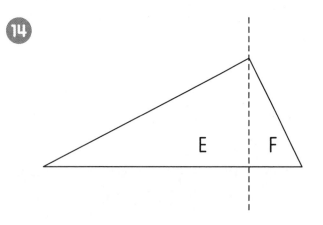

Shapes E and F _____

**Look at the triangle.**
**Then, circle the correct answer for each sentence.**

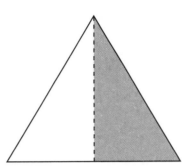

**15** The triangle is made up of | two | three | equal parts.

**16** One | half | quarter | of the triangle is shaded.

**Look at the circle.**
**Then, circle the correct answer for each sentence.**

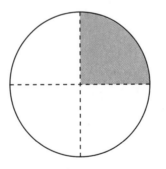

**17** The circle is made up of | three | four | equal parts.

**18** One | half | quarter | of the circle is shaded.

**Which rectangle is cut into halves?**
**Circle "A" or "B."**

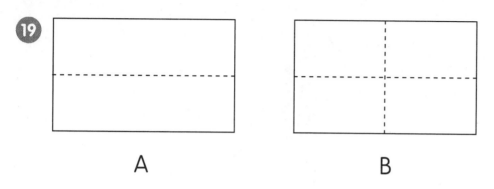

**19**

A

B

**Fill in the blank.**

**20** Which rectangle, A or B, in Question **19** has bigger parts?

Rectangle _____ has bigger parts.

**Color one quarter of the circle.**

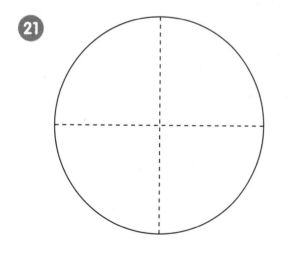

**21**

## Activity 2   Exploring Solid Shapes

**Match each shape to its name.**

**1**

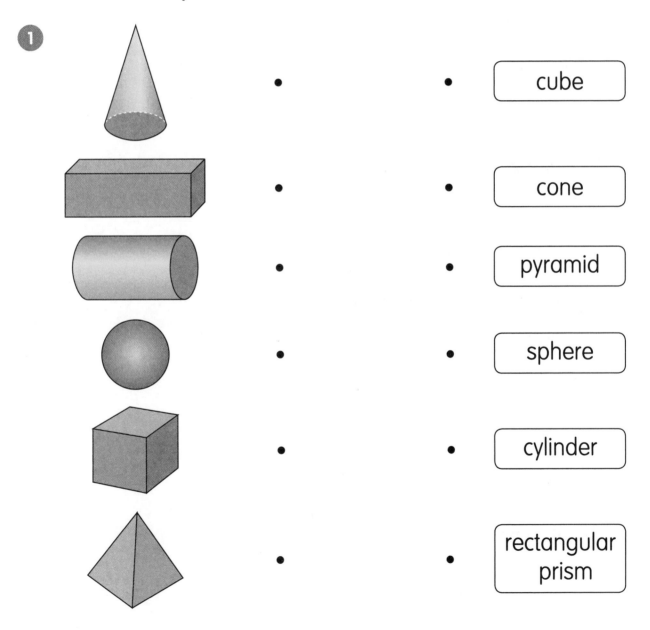

cube

cone

pyramid

sphere

cylinder

rectangular prism

## Which shapes are not cylinders?
## Circle them.

**2**

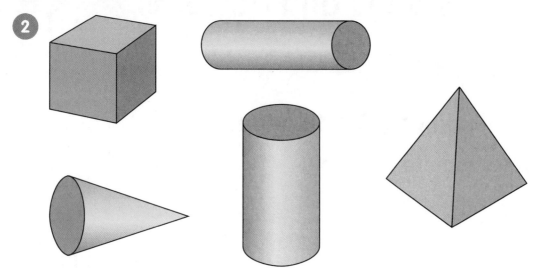

## Which shapes are not pyramids?
## Circle them.

**3**

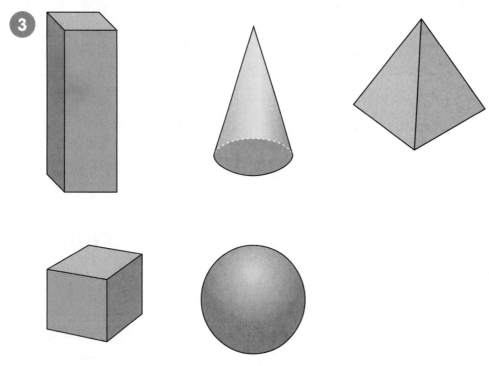

# Circle the shapes.

**4** Shapes you can stack

   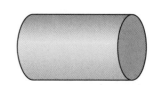

**5** Shapes you can slide

 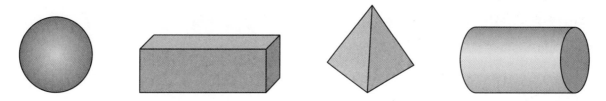

**6** Shapes you can roll

   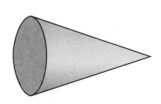

The shape you can roll and slide, but not stack

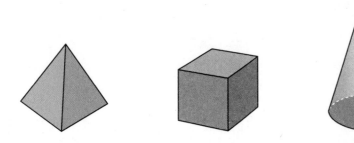

8 The shape you can roll, but not slide and stack

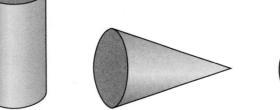

9 The only shape you can stack on itself

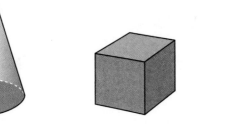

**Extra Practice and Homework**  Grade 1A

## Activity 3   Using Shapes to Make Pictures and Models

**Which shapes can you use to make the new shape?**
**Circle them.**

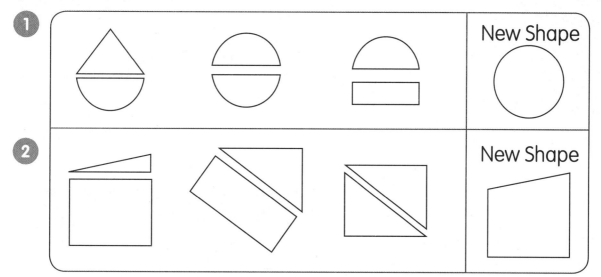

**Join the shapes shown.**
**Color the new shapes you can make.**

**Look at each picture.**
**Count each shape.**
**Then, fill in each table.**

**5**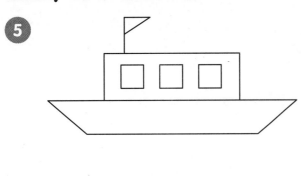

| Shape | | Number |
|:--|:--|:--|
| △ | Triangle | |
| ○ | Circle | |
| ▭ | Rectangle | |
| □ | Square | |
| ⬡ | Trapezoid | |

**6**

| Shape | | Number |
|:--|:--|:--|
| △ | Triangle | |
| ○ | Circle | |
| ▭ | Rectangle | |
| □ | Square | |
| ⬡ | Trapezoid | |

# Cut out the shapes below and make a picture.
# You do not need to use all the shapes.
# Paste the picture here.

**7**

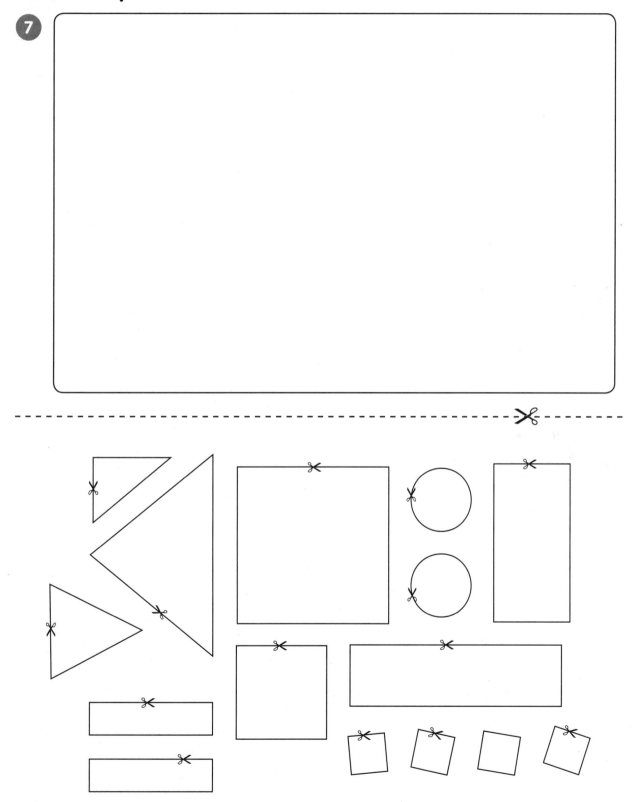

**Look at the table.**
**Use the shapes to draw a picture on your own paper.**
**Count each shape.**
**Fill in the table.**

8

| Shape | | Number |
|---|---|---|
| △ | Triangle | |
| ⏢ | Trapezoid | |
| ○ | Circle | |
| ▭ | Rectangle | |
| □ | Square | |

I can use a cup to draw a circle.

## Draw a line to show the shapes.

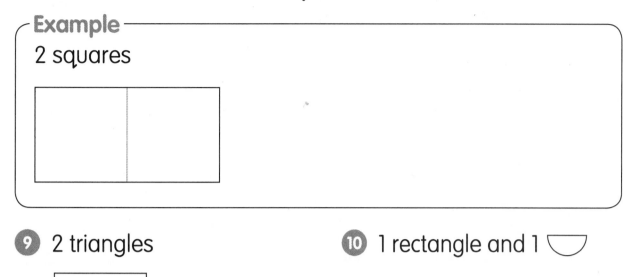

**Example**

2 squares

**9** 2 triangles

**10** 1 rectangle and 1 ⌣

## Look at the two solid shapes on the left.
## Color the new model you can make with them.

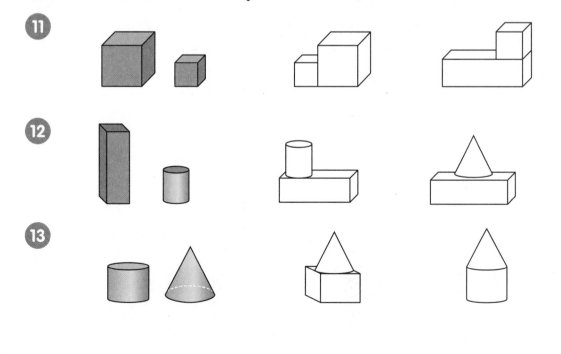

**11**

**12**

**13**

**Alan uses some solid shapes to build a tower.**
**Circle the solid shapes he uses.**

 Alan's Tower

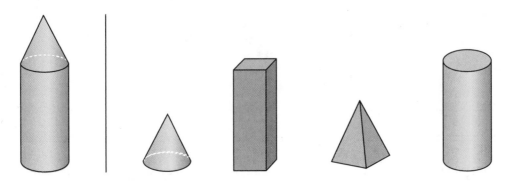

**Layla uses all the solid shapes to make a model.**
**Circle all the possible models.**

 15   2  and 2

16   2  and 2

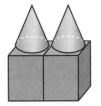

**Cole uses all the solid shapes to make a model.**
**Circle all the possible models.**

**17** 4 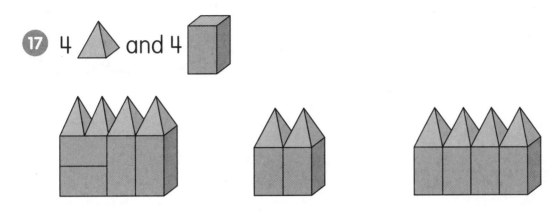 and 4

**Jasmine wants to build this model.**
**Color and count each of the solid shapes she needs.**
**Write your number in each blank.**

**18**

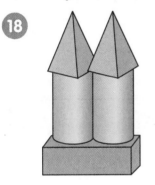

_____     _____     _____     _____

# Look at each picture.
# Count each solid shape.
# Fill in each table.

**19**

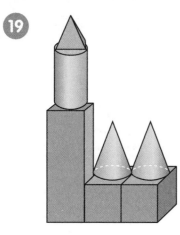

| Solid Shape | | Number |
|---|---|---|
| | Cylinder | |
| | Rectangular prism | |
| | Cone | |
| | Cube | |
| | Pyramid | |

**20**

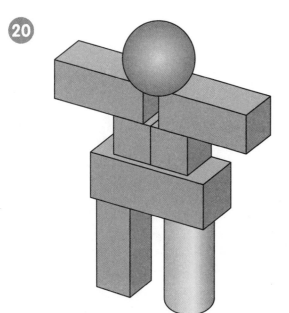

| Solid Shape | | Number |
|---|---|---|
| | Sphere | |
| | Cylinder | |
| | Rectangular prism | |
| | Cube | |
| | Pyramid | |

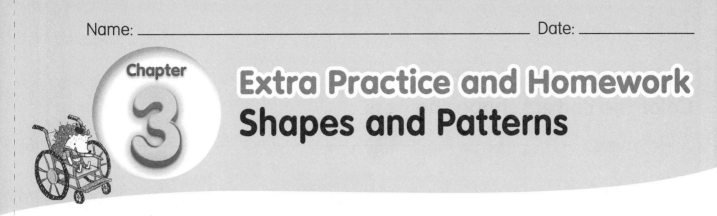

# Extra Practice and Homework
## Shapes and Patterns

## Activity 4   Seeing Shapes Around Us

Trace the shape of each object.
Then, color each object in the correct color.

**1**

| | | | |
|---|---|---|---|
| ● | Circles in red | ▬ | Rectangles in green |
| ▲ | Triangles in blue | ▽ | Trapezoids in orange |
| ■ | Squares in yellow | | |

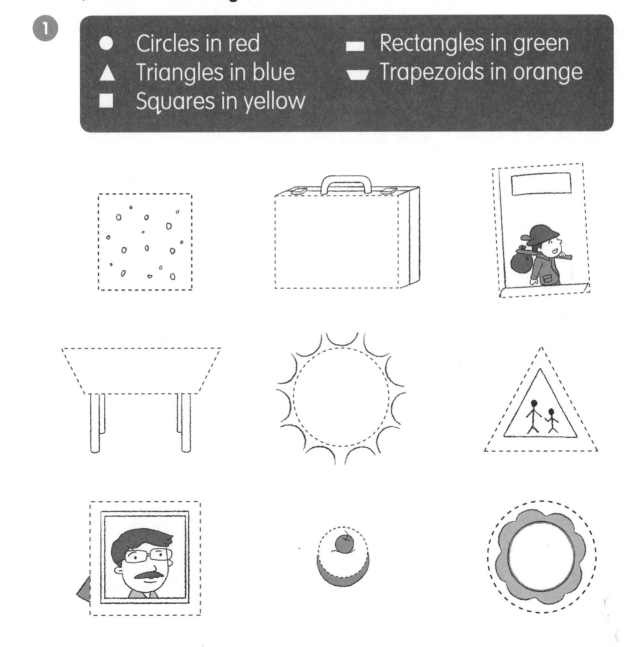

# Sara traces each object.
# Color the correct shape she gets.

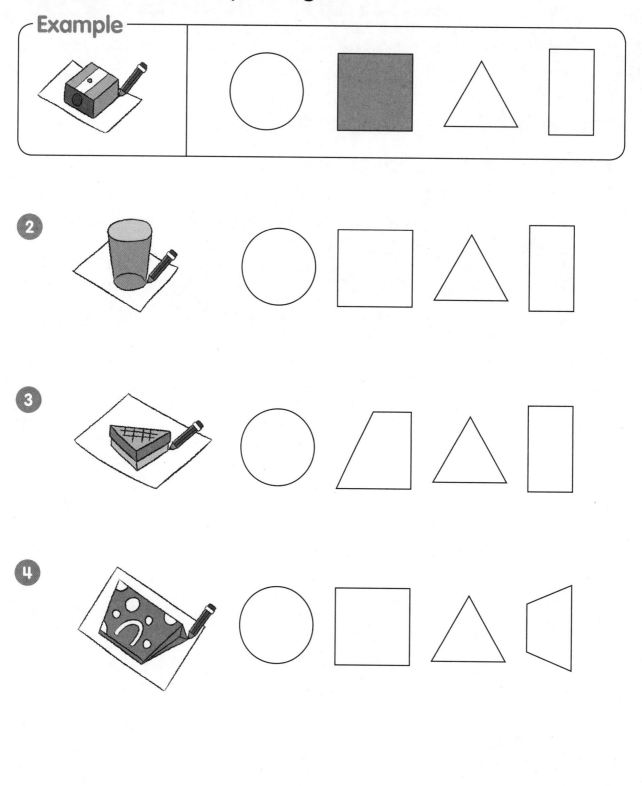

# Look at each picture.
# Match each picture to its flat shape and solid shape.

**5**

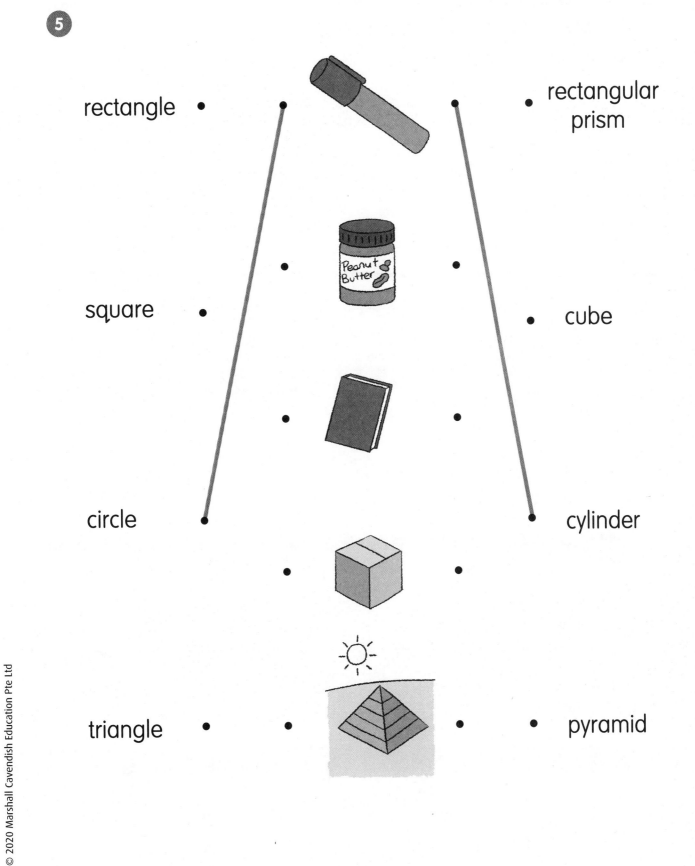

rectangle

square

circle

triangle

rectangular prism

cube

cylinder

pyramid

# Look at the picture.
# Color the shapes in the correct color.
# Then, answer the question.

**6**

| Shape | Color | Shape | Color |
|-------|-------|-------|-------|
| Cube | Blue | Pyramid | Purple |
| Sphere | Red | Rectangular prism | Green |
| Cone | Yellow | Cylinder | Orange |

What shape is not in the picture? _____

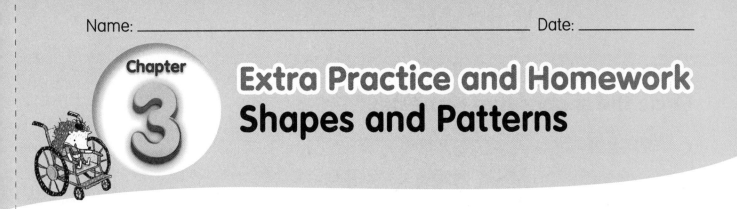

### Chapter 3

# Extra Practice and Homework
## Shapes and Patterns

## Activity 5   Using Flat Shapes to Make Patterns

Look at each pattern.
Circle the shape that comes next.

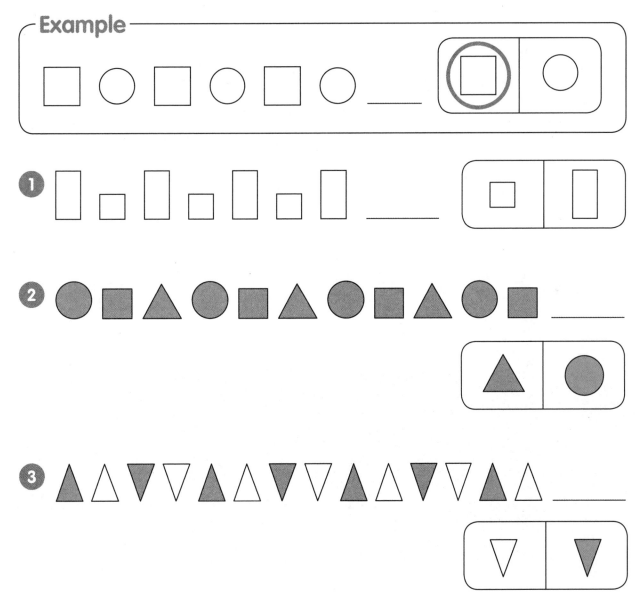

# Look at each pattern.
# Circle the shapes that come next.

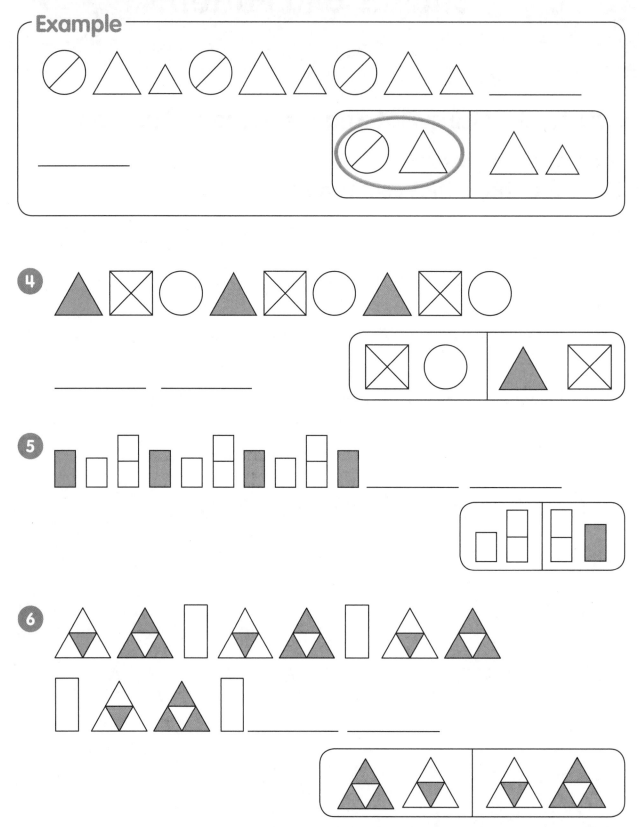

# Cut out the shapes below.
# Make two patterns with a change in color or shape.
# You do not need to use all the shapes.

**7** Paste your first pattern here.

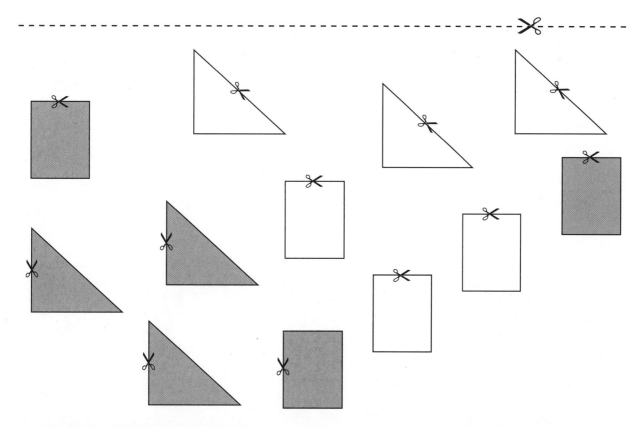

Paste your second pattern here.

✂ - - - - - - - - - - - - - - - - - - - - - - - - - - - - - - - - - - - - - - - - - - - - -

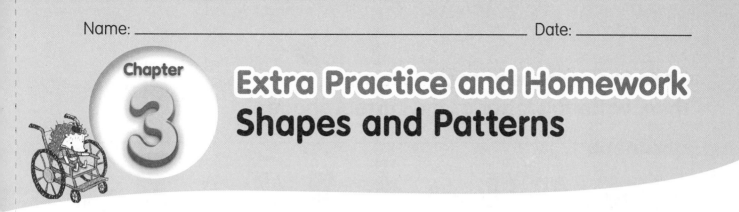

**Chapter 3**

# Extra Practice and Homework
# Shapes and Patterns

## Activity 6    Using Solid Shapes to Make Patterns

Look at each pattern.
Circle the solid shape that comes next.

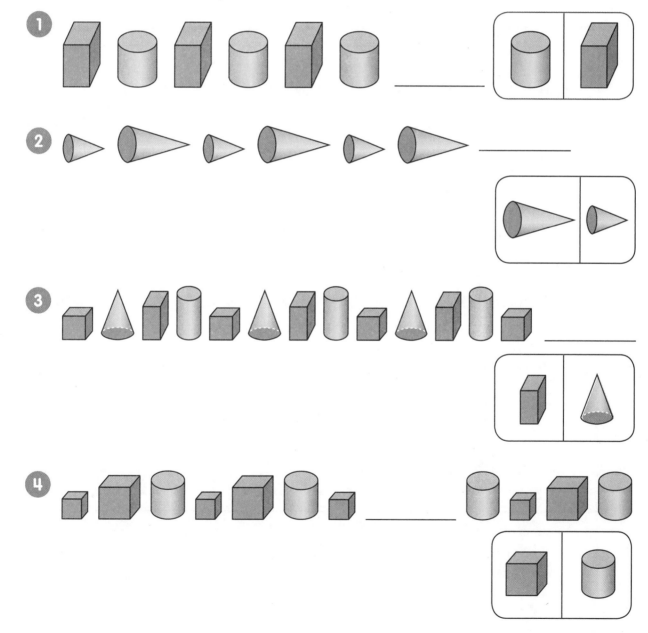

# Circle the mistake in each pattern.
# Then, write the letter of the correct shape.

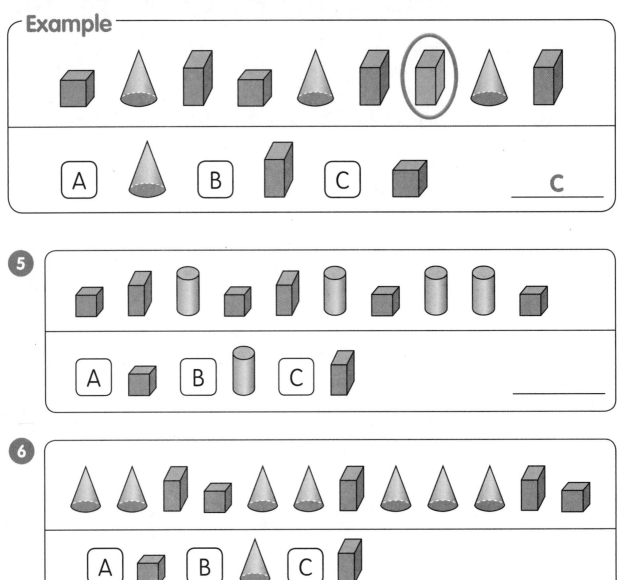

**Example**

A    B    C

C

5

A    B    C

_____

6

A    B    C

_____

7

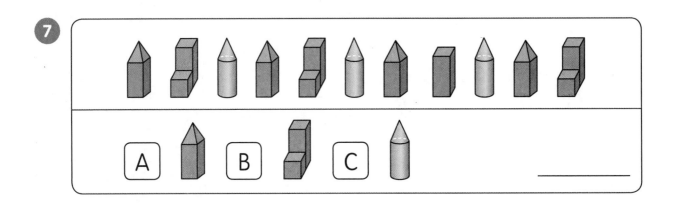

A    B    C

_____

Name: _____ Date: _____

**1** **Mathematical Habit 6** **Use precise mathematical language**

**a** Choose two objects.
Circle them.

ball          sharpener          soap          party hat

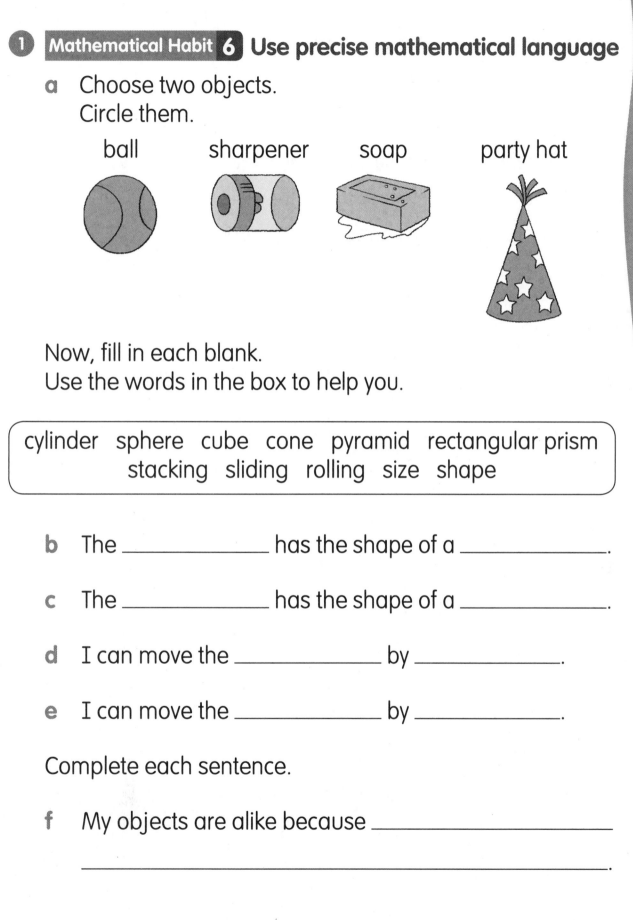

Now, fill in each blank.
Use the words in the box to help you.

> cylinder   sphere   cube   cone   pyramid   rectangular prism
> stacking   sliding   rolling   size   shape

**b** The _____ has the shape of a _____.

**c** The _____ has the shape of a _____.

**d** I can move the _____ by _____.

**e** I can move the _____ by _____.

Complete each sentence.

**f** My objects are alike because _____

_____.

**g**   My objects are different because _____

_____.

**2**   Read the sentences and draw this pattern.

- The shapes in this pattern are flat.
- The shapes in this pattern are alike.
- The sizes of the shapes are different.

**1** **Mathematical Habit 2** **Use mathematical reasoning**

Ava, Brody, Diego, and Ethan have some shapes.

Find out who has each set of shapes.

- Ava has fewer circles than Diego.
- All of Brody's shapes have three or four sides.
- Diego has four kinds of shapes.
- Ethan has no squares.

Write the name that matches each set.

_____ _____

_____ _____

② **Mathematical Habit 7 Make use of structure**

Cut out the shapes on the next page.
Paste the cut-out shapes to fit each picture below.

a

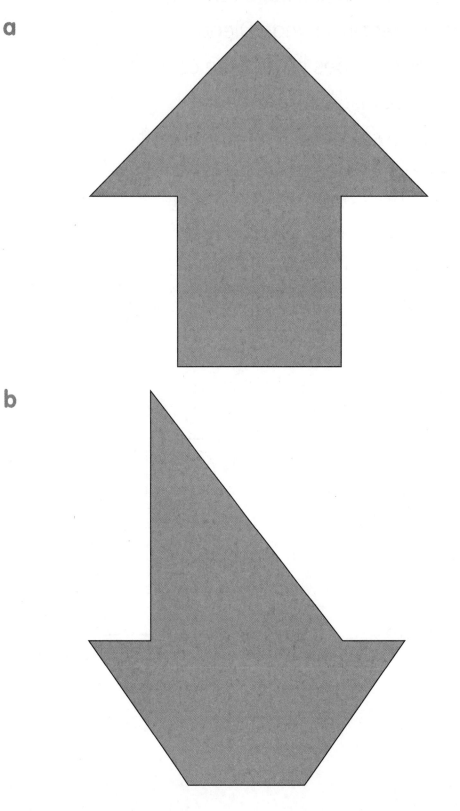

b

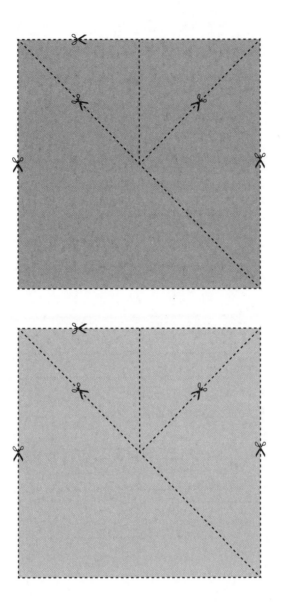

BLANK

# SCHOOL-to-HOME
## CONNECTIONS

## Numbers to 20

## Dear Family,

In this chapter, your child will work with numbers to 20. Skills your child will practice include:

- counting on from 10 to 20
- reading and writing 11 to 20 in numbers and words
- using a place-value chart to show numbers to 20
- comparing and ordering numbers to 20
- finding missing numbers in a number pattern

### Math Practice

At the end of this chapter, you may want to carry out these activities with your child. These activities will help to strengthen your child's number sense.

### Activity 1

- Write the numbers 1 to 20 on separate cards.
- Shuffle the cards and put them facedown.
- Ask your child to select a card and read the number aloud while you do the same.
- Have your child identify whether his or her number is greater than or less than your number.
- Repeat the activity several times.

### Activity 2

- Write the numbers 1 to 20 on separate cards.
- Write the questions "Which number is greater?" and "Which number is less?" on separate cards.
- Shuffle the number cards and put them face down.
- Shuffle the question cards and put them face down.
- Select two number cards and read the numbers aloud.
- Select a question card and read the question aloud.
- Use the number cards to answer the question in the question card.
- Return the cards before your child leads the next round.

### Math Talk

Use the following example to discuss with your child how to compare numbers. Use the words **greater than** and **less than** in your discussion.

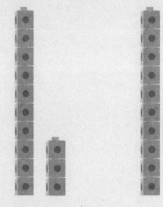

13 is greater than 10.

10 is less than 13.

BLANK

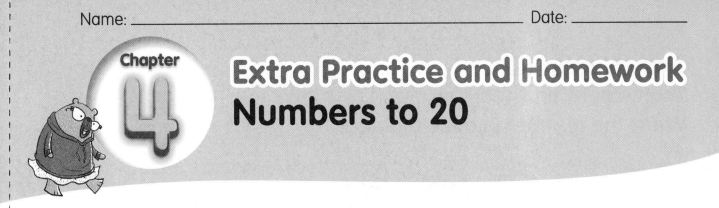

## Chapter 4

# Extra Practice and Homework
# Numbers to 20

## Activity 1   Counting to 20

**Count.**
**Write the number in each blank.**

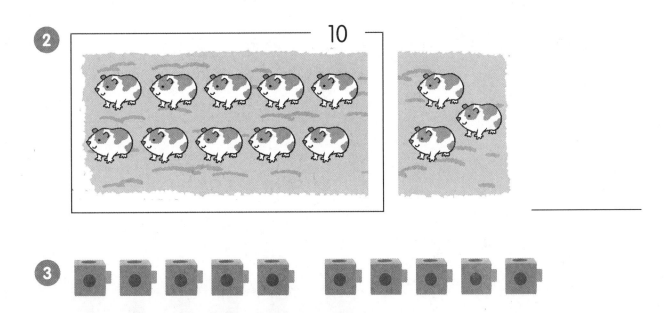

**1**    10

_____

**2**    10

_____

**3**

_____

# Circle to make a 10.
## Then, count on.
## Write the number in each blank.

**4**

_____

**5**

_____

**6**

_____

**Extra Practice and Homework** Grade 1A

## Fill in each blank.

**7** 

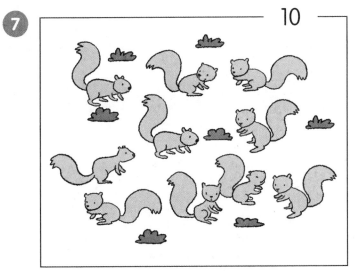 

10

10 and 3 make _____.     10 + 3 = _____

**8**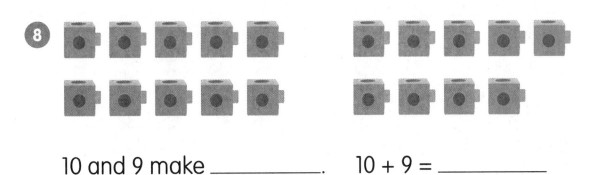

10 and 9 make _____.     10 + 9 = _____

**9** 10 and 2 make _____.

10 + 2 = _____

**10** 10 and 7 make _____.

_____ + _____ = _____

# Circle to make a 10.
# Then, count on.
# Write each number and word.

**11**

Number _____  Word _____

**12**

Number _____  Word _____

**13**

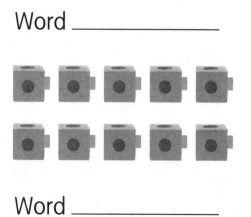

Number _____  Word _____

## Unscramble each word.
## Then, write each word and number.

**Example**

| | Word | Number |
|---|---|---|
| teeeihng | eighteen | 18 |

| | | Word | Number |
|---|---|---|---|
| 14 | neeffti | _____tee__ | |
| 15 | xstinee | __i_____en | |
| 16 | eenvel | _____even | |

## Match.

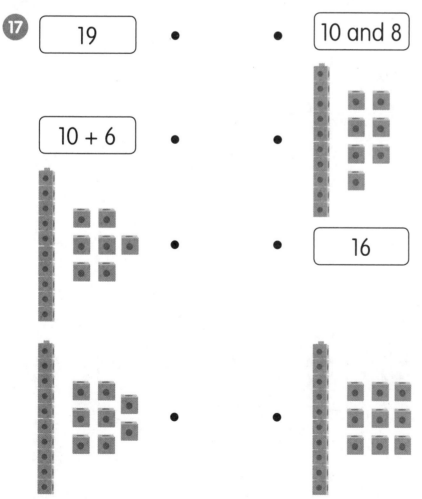

17  19  •        •  10 and 8

10 + 6  •        •  16

**There is a mistake in each puzzle.**
**Find the mistake and circle it.**
**Then, correct the mistake in each puzzle.**

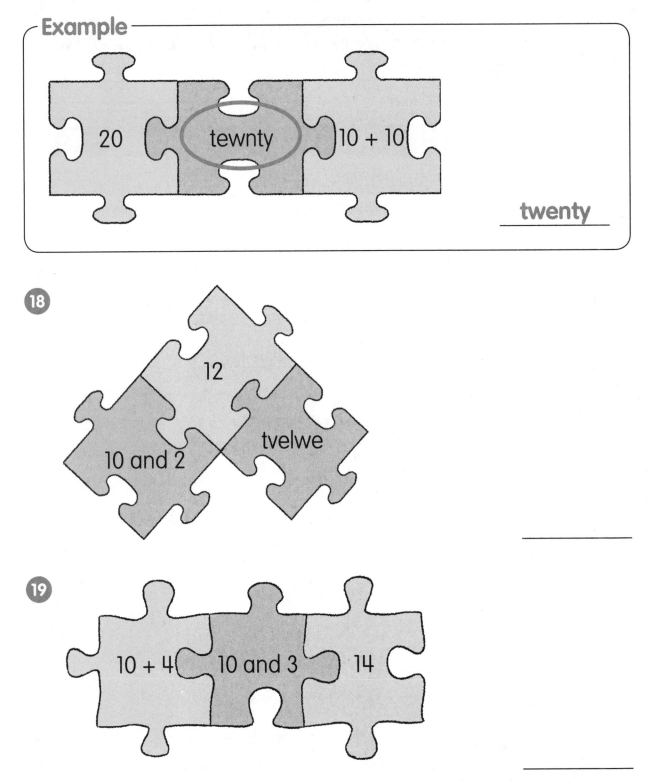

**Example**

20 | (tewnty) | 10 + 10

twenty

**18**

12

10 and 2

tvelwe

_____

**19**

10 + 4 | 10 and 3 | 14

_____

**Extra Practice and Homework** Grade 1A

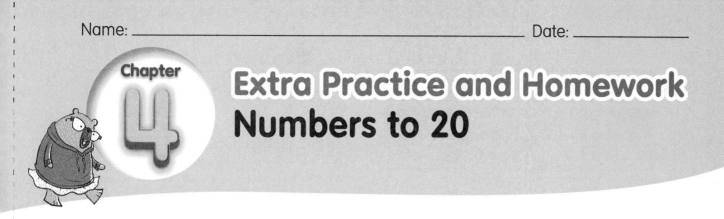

## Activity 2   Place Value

**Write each missing number.**

**1**

_____ ten _____ ones

| Tens | Ones |
|------|------|
|      |      |

**Look at each place-value chart.**
**Does the number of 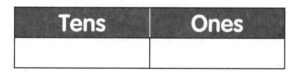 and ⬡ match the number below them?**
**Color the box with the correct statement.**

**2**

| Tens | Ones |
|------|------|
| 1    | 1    |

| The pair matches. |
|---|
| The pair does not match. |

**3**

| Tens | Ones |
|------|------|
| 1    | 7    |

| The pair matches. |
|---|
| The pair does not match. |

**4**

| Tens | Ones |
|------|------|
| 1 | 5 |

The pair matches.

The pair does not match.

## Write each missing number.

**5** 20 = 2 tens _____ ones

**6** _____ = 1 ten 1 one

## Match.

**7**

•

| Tens | Ones |
|------|------|
| 1 | 3 |

•

| Tens | Ones |
|------|------|
| 1 | 2 |

•

| Tens | Ones |
|------|------|
| 1 | 6 |

•

| Tens | Ones |
|------|------|
| 1 | 8 |

## Count the eggs.
## Write the number in the blank.

**8**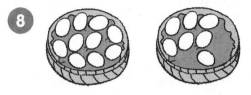

_____

## Which show the same number?
## Circle the ones that do.

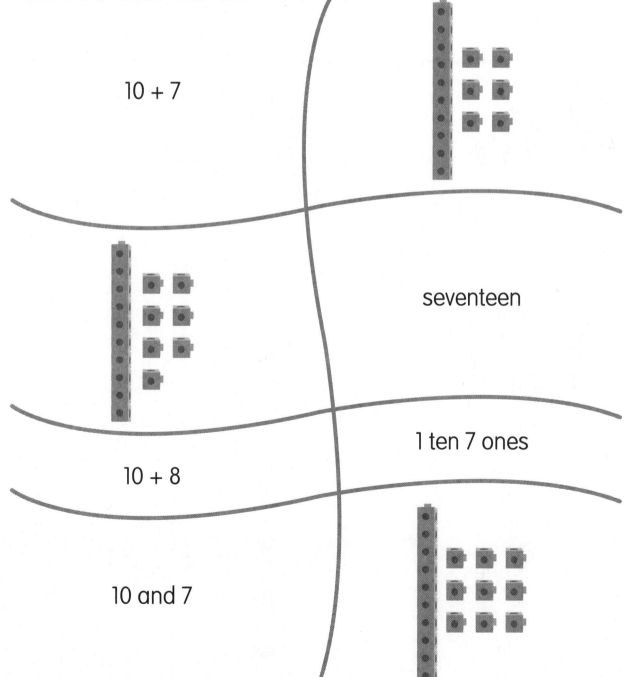

10 + 7

seventeen

1 ten 7 ones

10 + 8

10 and 7

## Match.

**9**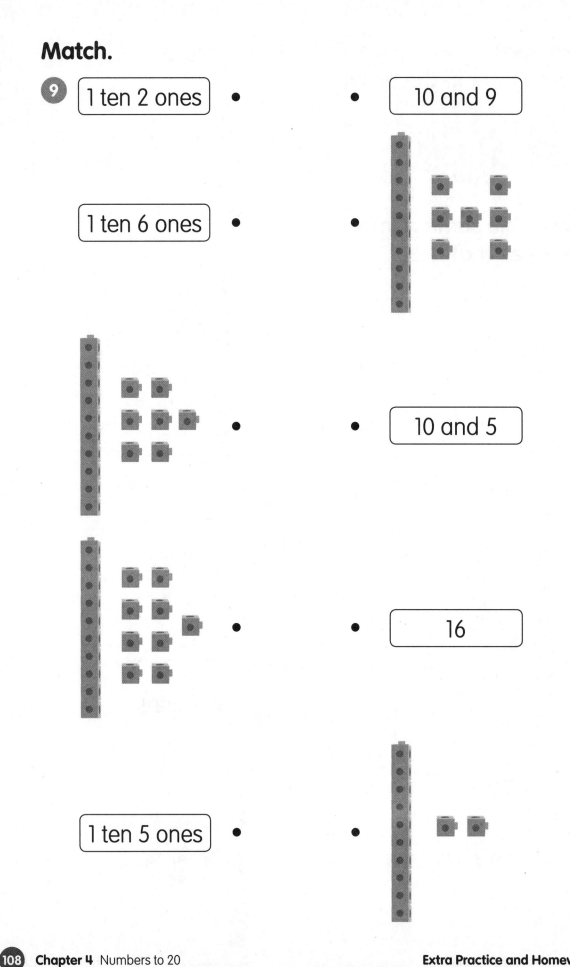

1 ten 2 ones •          • 10 and 9

1 ten 6 ones •          • 

•          • 10 and 5

•          • 16

1 ten 5 ones •          •

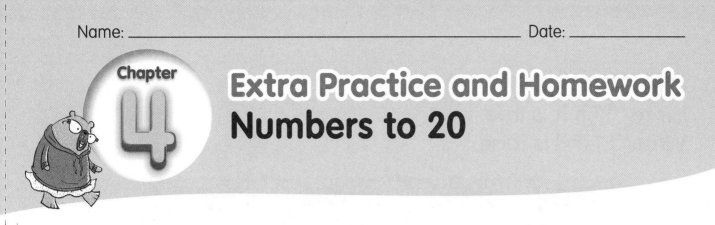

## Chapter 4

# Extra Practice and Homework
# Numbers to 20

## Activity 3   Comparing and Ordering Numbers

**Circle the number that is greater.**
**Cross out (✗) the number that is less.**

Example

(12)  ✗10✗

1   13   16

2   18   20

3   19   16

**Look at each statement.**
**Write "T" if it is true.**
**Write "F" if it is false.**

4  12 < 16  _____

5  19 > 20  _____

6  16 > 19  _____

7  20 > 16  _____

8  20 > 12  _____

9  19 < 12  _____

**Fill in each blank with ">" or "<."**

10

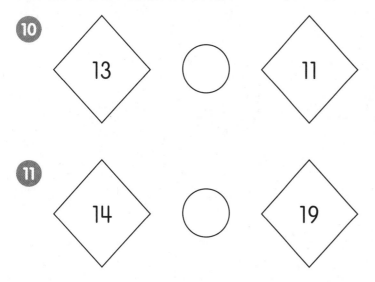

13   ◯   11

11

14   ◯   19

**Look at the numbers in each group.**
**Are they in order from least to greatest?**
**Circle "Yes" or "No."**

12

Yes / No

13

Yes / No

**Compare the numbers.**
**Then, fill in each blank.**

14 _____ is the greatest number.

15 _____ is the least number.

## Order the numbers from least to greatest.

**16**

_____, _____, _____

least                     greatest

## Order the numbers from greatest to least.

**17**

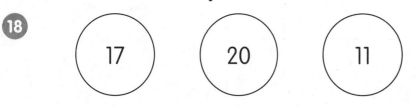

_____, _____, _____

greatest                 least

## Look at the numbers.
## Then, answer each question.

**18**

( 17 )      ( 20 )      ( 11 )

a   Are the numbers in order from least to greatest?

_____

b   Which two numbers can you swap to order from greatest to least?
Underline them.

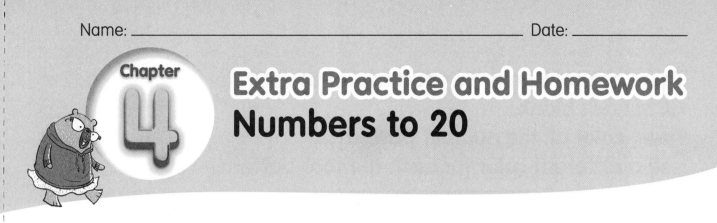

## Chapter 4

# Extra Practice and Homework
# Numbers to 20

## Activity 4   Number Patterns

**Write the missing numbers in each number pattern.**

**1** 14, 13, 12, 11, _____, _____, _____

**2** 16, _____,14, 13, 12, 11, _____

**3** 20, 19, 18, 17, _____, 15, _____

**Look at the given numbers.**
**Use them to make two different number patterns.**
**You may use a number more than once.**

**4**

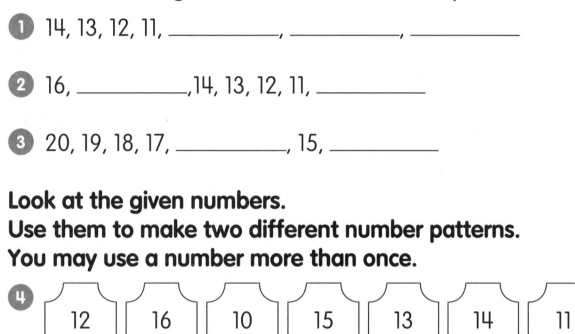

| 12 | 16 | 10 | 15 | 13 | 14 | 11 |

Pattern 1:

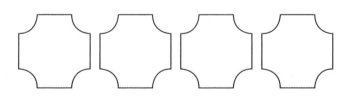

Pattern 2:

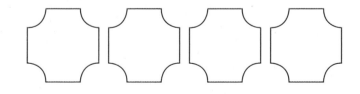

There are some number patterns in the puzzle.
Fill in each blank.
Then, color all the number patterns.
Use a different color for each number pattern.

**5**

| 17 | 19 | 18 | 8 | 13 | 14 | 17 |
|----|----|----|----|----|----|----|
| 12 | 15 | 16 | 12 | 14 | 16 | 15 |
| 10 | 11 | 14 | 17 | 15 | 13 | 14 |
| 8 | 10 | 12 | 14 | 16 |  | 20 |
| 6 | 5 |  | 11 |  | 15 | 18 |
| 4 | 1 | 8 | 7 | 18 | 10 | 14 |
| 2 | 5 | 6 | 13 | 19 | 12 | 16 |

**MATH JOURNAL**

**1** **Mathematical Habit 6** **Use precise mathematical language**

Choose any of these numbers.

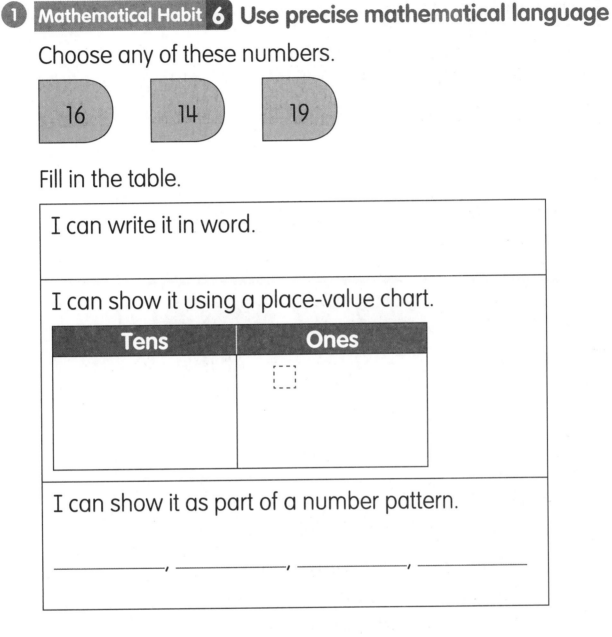

16    14    19

Fill in the table.

| I can write it in word. |
| --- |
|  |

I can show it using a place-value chart.

| Tens | Ones |
| --- | --- |
|  | [ ] |

I can show it as part of a number pattern.

_____, _____, _____, _____

**2** | **Mathematical Habit 2** | **Use mathematical reasoning**

Look at the problem and the table.
The steps in the table to work out the problem are mixed up.
Number them in the correct order.

Problem:
Order the numbers from greatest to least.

14    20    19

| The steps: | |
|---|---|
|  | 20 has 2 tens.<br>2 tens are greater than 1 ten. |
|  | 4 ones are less than 9 ones.<br>So, 14 is less than 19.<br>14 is the least number. |
|  | The greatest number is 20. |
| 1 | Compare the tens. |
|  | 20,    19,    14<br>greatest        least |
|  | Now, compare the ones in 19 and 14. |
|  | 14 and 19 each has 1 ten. |

© 2020 Marshall Cavendish Education Pte Ltd

**1** **Mathematical Habit 1** **Persevere in solving problems**

Anya practices writing numbers from 1 to 20.

After writing 19 digits, she stops and takes a rest.
Find the number Anya stops at.

Numbers like 10, 11, 12 and so on have two digits. I must be careful.

**2** | **Mathematical Habit** **1** **Persevere in solving problems**

Read the clue.
Then, circle the correct numbers.

Clue:
The numbers are greater than 13, but less than 18.

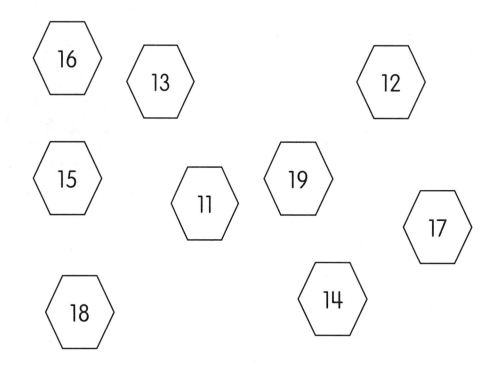

## Chapter 5
# Addition and Subtraction Within 20

## Dear Family,

In this chapter, your child will add and subtract within 20. Skills your child will practice include:

- adding by counting on
- adding by making a 10
- adding by using doubles and doubles plus one facts
- subtracting by counting back
- subtracting by grouping into a 10 and ones
- subtracting by using addition facts
- solving real-world problems involving addition and subtraction

## Math Practice

At the end of this chapter, you may want to carry out these activities with your child. These activities will help to strengthen your child's understanding of addition and subtraction within 20.

## Activity 1

- Gather a paper plate, a number cube, and 20 identical objects, such as dried beans, macaroni shells, or buttons.
- Put up to 14 objects on the plate and count aloud as you do so.
- Roll the number cube and put the corresponding number of objects on the plate, counting on to find the total number of objects.
- Empty the plate and let your child lead the next round.

## Activity 2

- Gather a paper plate, a number cube, and 20 identical objects, such as dried beans, macaroni shells, or buttons.
- Put 20 objects on the plate and count aloud as you put them on the plate.
- Roll the number cube and remove the corresponding number of objects from the plate, counting back to find the number of objects that remain.
- Empty the plate and let your child lead the next round.

### Math Talk

Use the following diagram to help your child recall how a number bond shows the relationship between a whole number and its parts. For example, the parts 1 and 6 form a number bond for 7.

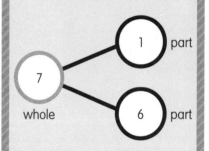

Next, look at the following diagram with your child. Encourage your child to make 10 first before adding or subtracting. Ask your child to break the number that is less up into two parts.

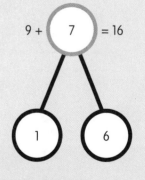

9 and 1 make 10.
10 and 6 make 16.

**BLANK**

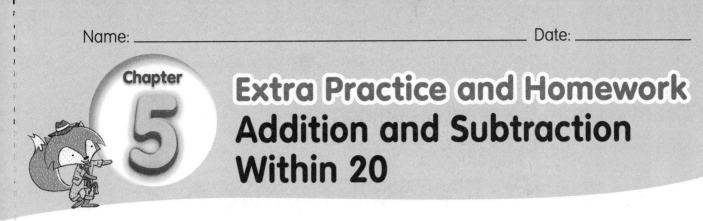

# Chapter 5 Extra Practice and Homework
## Addition and Subtraction Within 20

## Activity 1    Ways to Add Fluently

**Add.**
**Count on from the greater number.**
**Fill in each missing number.**

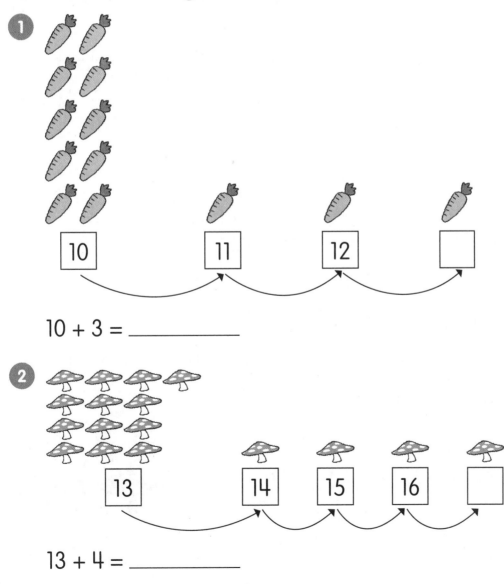

**1**

| 10 | 11 | 12 | |

10 + 3 = _____

**2**

| 13 | 14 | 15 | 16 | |

13 + 4 = _____

# Add.
## Count on from the greater number.
## Use the counting tape to help you.

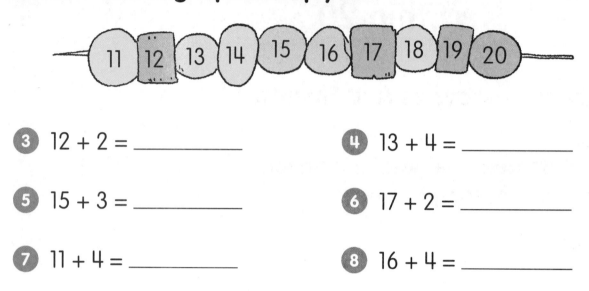

**3** 12 + 2 = _____

**4** 13 + 4 = _____

**5** 15 + 3 = _____

**6** 17 + 2 = _____

**7** 11 + 4 = _____

**8** 16 + 4 = _____

# Make a 10.
## Then, add and fill in each blank.

**9**

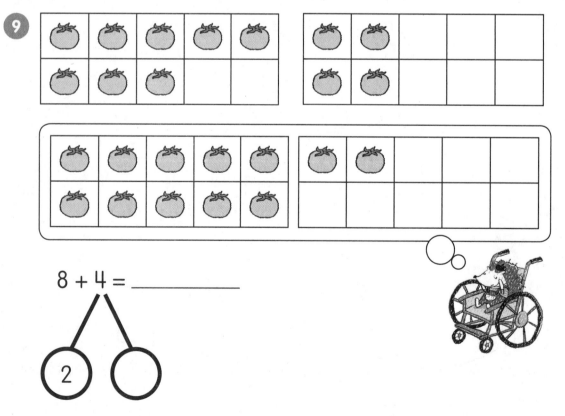

8 + 4 = _____

**Extra Practice and Homework** Grade 1A

**10**

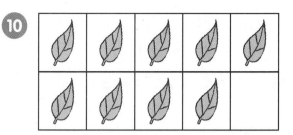

$9 + 9 = \underline{\hspace{2cm}}$

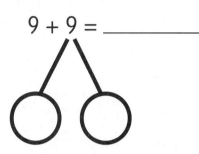

## Make a 10.
## Then, add and fill in each blank.

**11**    $7 + 6 = \underline{\hspace{2cm}}$

**12**    $7 + 8 = \underline{\hspace{2cm}}$

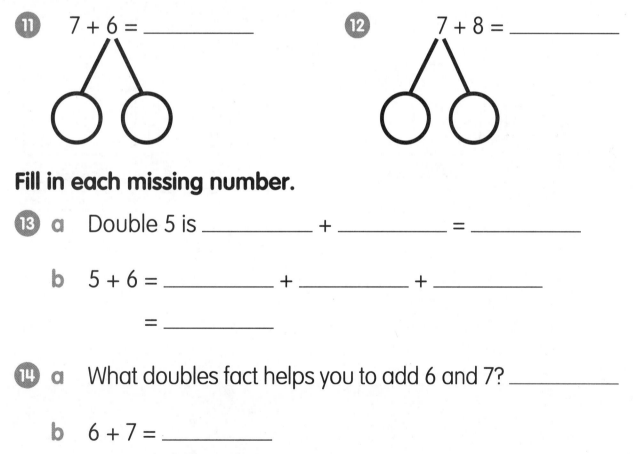

## Fill in each missing number.

**13**   a   Double 5 is $\underline{\hspace{2cm}} + \underline{\hspace{2cm}} = \underline{\hspace{2cm}}$

    b   $5 + 6 = \underline{\hspace{2cm}} + \underline{\hspace{2cm}} + \underline{\hspace{2cm}}$

           $= \underline{\hspace{2cm}}$

**14**   a   What doubles fact helps you to add 6 and 7? $\underline{\hspace{2cm}}$

    b   $6 + 7 = \underline{\hspace{2cm}}$

**Which two buses can take Pablo home?**
**Add up each pair of numbers for the bus number.**
**Then, read the clues to help Pablo find these buses.**
**Circle these buses.**

15

$4 + 4$

= _____

$8 + 7$

= _____

$3 + 9$

= _____

$13 + 7$

= _____

$9 + 5$

= _____

Clues:

Hello! Do you know which buses can take my family and I to this place?

Pablo

Oh! Sorry, I need to hurry! Do not take buses with 1 in the tens place.

Golden Meadows Street 21

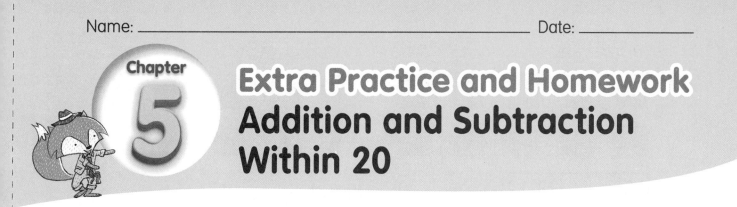

### Chapter 5 Extra Practice and Homework
# Addition and Subtraction Within 20

## Activity 2  Ways to Subtract Fluently

**Subtract.**
**Count back from the greater number.**
**Draw arrows to help you.**
**Then, fill in each missing number.**

1

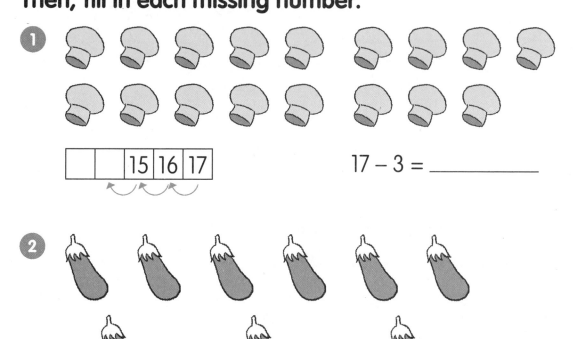

| | | 15 | 16 | 17 |
|---|---|---|---|---|

17 − 3 = _____

2

| | | 12 | 13 | 14 | 15 |
|---|---|---|---|---|---|

15 − 4 = _____

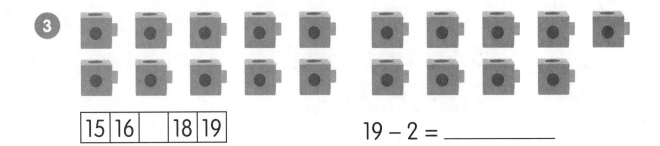

**3**

| 15 | 16 |  | 18 | 19 |

$19 - 2 =$ _____

## Subtract.
## Count back from the greater number.
## Use the counting tape to help you.

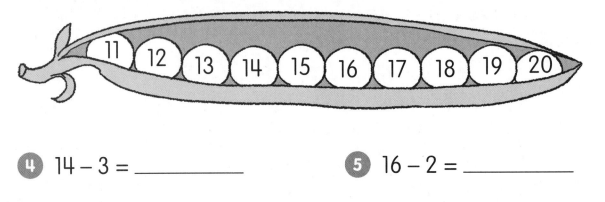

**4** $14 - 3 =$ _____

**5** $16 - 2 =$ _____

**6** $17 - 1 =$ _____

**7** $20 - 4 =$ _____

## Group each number into a 10 and ones.
## Then, subtract and fill in each blank.

**8**

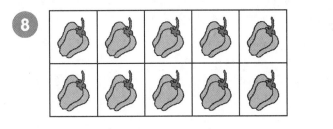 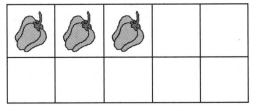

$13 - 3 =$ _____

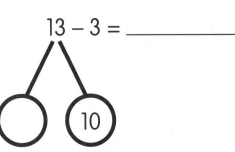

**9**

$$20 - 5 = \underline{\hspace{3cm}}$$

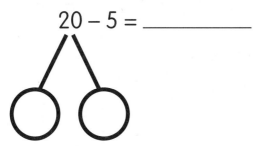

**10**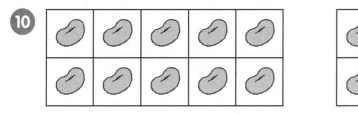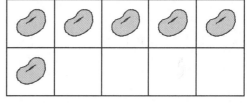

$$16 - 7 = \underline{\hspace{3cm}}$$

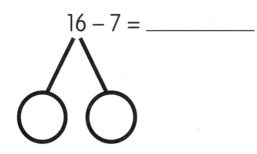

**Group each number into a 10 and ones.**
**Then, subtract and fill in each blank.**

**11**     $17 - 4 = \underline{\hspace{3cm}}$

**12**     $13 - 5 = \underline{\hspace{3cm}}$

**Subtract.**

13   12 – 3 = _____

14   13 – 4 = _____

15   14 – 6 = _____

16   16 – 8 = _____

**Subtract.**
**Use a related addition fact to help you.**
**Write the related addition fact.**

17   15 – 6 = _____

     Addition fact: _____ + _____ = _____

18   14 – 8 = _____

     Addition fact: _____ + _____ = _____

**Look at each number sentence.**
**Is it true or false?**
**Fill in each blank to find out.**

19   14 – 4 = 8 + 3

     14 – 4 = _____          8 + 3 = _____

     14 – 4 = 8 + 3 is _____ (true/false).

20   15 – 7 = 11 – 3

     15 – 7 = _____          11 – 3 = _____

     15 – 7 = 11 – 3 is _____ (true/false).

# Chapter 5
# Extra Practice and Homework
## Addition and Subtraction Within 20

### Activity 3 Real-World Problems: Addition and Subtraction

**Solve.**

1. Michael has 9 toy cars.
   He has 7 toy trucks.
   How many trucks and cars does Michael have in all?

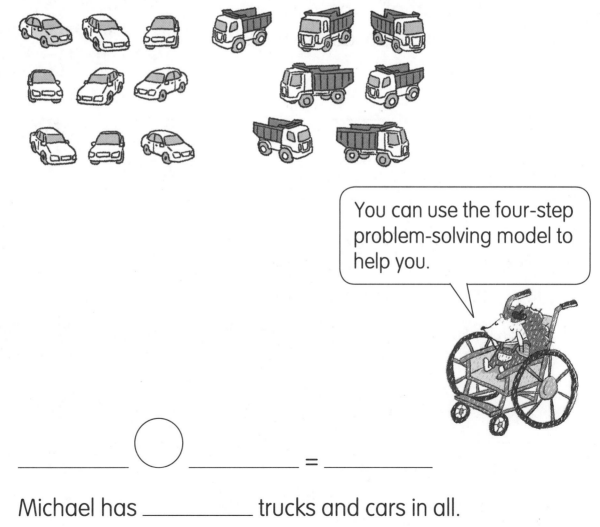

You can use the four-step problem-solving model to help you.

_____ ◯ _____ = _____

Michael has _____ trucks and cars in all.

**2** Ms. Evans has 12 cookbooks.
She buys 7 cookbooks.
How many cookbooks does Ms. Evans have now?

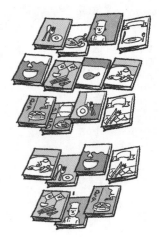

_____ ◯ _____ = _____

Ms. Evans has _____ cookbooks now.

**3** Mr. Lee gives his wife 16 roses.
7 roses are big ones.
The rest are small ones.
How many small roses are there?

_____ ◯ _____ = _____

There are _____ small roses.

**4** There are 11 ladybugs on a leaf.
A bird eats 3 of the ladybugs.
How many ladybugs are there left?

_____ ◯ _____ = _____

There are _____ ladybugs left.

**5** Tomas gives away 10 stickers to his friends.
He also gives his sister 3 stickers.
How many stickers does Tomas give away in all?

_____ ◯ _____ = _____

Tomas gives away _____ stickers in all.

**6** Angel makes 20 bracelets.
She gives away some bracelets.
She has 8 bracelets now.
How many bracelets does Angel give away?

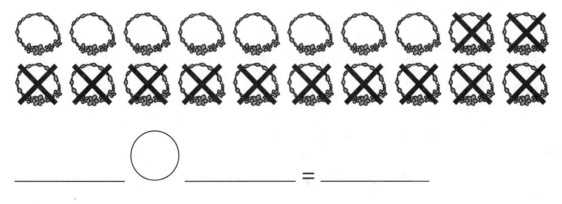

_____ ◯ _____ = _____

Angel gives away _____ bracelets.

**7** Ms. Brown has 6 cups.
She buys some cups.
Ms. Brown has 11 cups now.
How many cups does Ms. Brown buy?

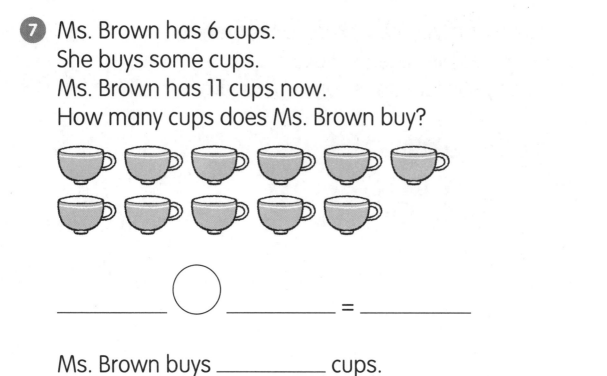

_____ ◯ _____ = _____

Ms. Brown buys _____ cups.

**8** There are 18 big and small ants on a leaf.
There are 8 big ants.
How many small ants are there?

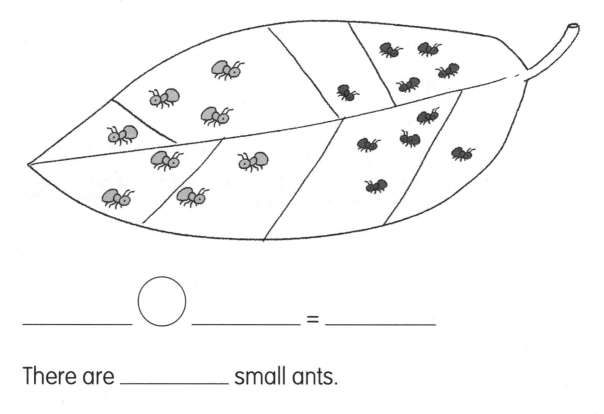

_____ ◯ _____ = _____

There are _____ small ants.

Name: _____ Date: _____

## Mathematical Habit 4 Use mathematical models

Color the ☐ to show five different ways to make 20.

### Way 1

### Way 2

### Way 3

### Way 4

### Way 5

**1** | Mathematical Habit **1** **Persevere in solving problems**

Fill in each ◯ with one of the numbers from the table.

You can only use each number once.

| 4 | 9 | 8 | 6 |
|---|---|---|---|
| 12 | 7 | 11 | 3 |

Each of the ◯—⑤—◯ in the directions →, ↓, ↗,

and ↘ must make 20.

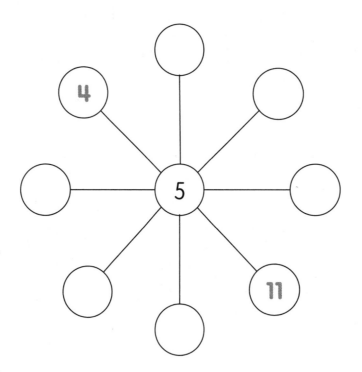

**Extra Practice and Homework** Grade 1A

**2** **Mathematical Habit** **1** **Persevere in solving problems**

There are four letters in the code to open the cave door.
What is the missing letter?

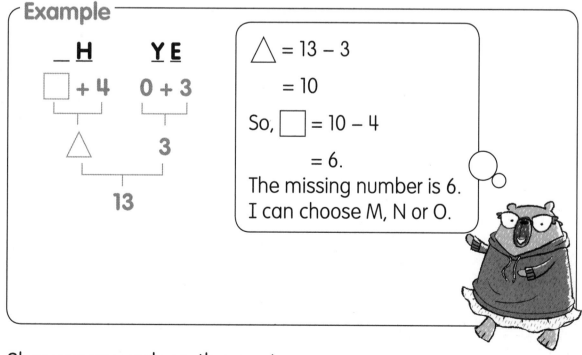

**Example**

_ **H**           **Y E**

☐ + 4      0 + 3

△          3

13

△ = 13 − 3
  = 10
So, ☐ = 10 − 4
  = 6.
The missing number is 6.
I can choose M, N or O.

Show your work on the next page.

**BLANK**

# SCHOOL-to-HOME
## CONNECTIONS

**Chapter 6**

## Numbers to 40

## Dear Family,

In this chapter, your child will work with numbers to 40. Skills your child will practice include:

- counting on from 20 to 40
- representing a number of objects with a written number and word.
- using a place-value chart to show numbers to 40
- comparing and ordering numbers to 40
- finding missing numbers in a number pattern

## Math Practice

At the end of this chapter, you may want to carry out this activity with your child. This activity will help to strengthen your child's number sense.

## Activity

- Gather 40 identical objects such as dried beans or macaroni, buttons, or plastic cubes and put the objects in a bag.
- Pull out a large handful of objects and ask your child to count them, starting with groups of 10. Your child can move objects to make groups of 10 or loop string around groups of 10. If the objects are scattered on a sheet of paper, draw circles around groups of 10 to make counting easier.
- Return all the objects to the bag before the next round.

### Math Talk

Discuss with your child how each digit in a number is in a particular position, or place, and that place determines a digit's value. Look at the following place-value chart together, and talk about how to write 24 as 2 groups of 10 and 4 ones, or 10 + 10 + 4.

| Tens | Ones |
|------|------|
| 2    | 4    |

**BLANK**

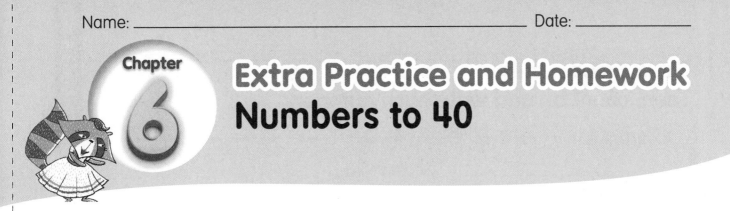

# Extra Practice and Homework
# Numbers to 40

## Activity 1   Counting to 40

Count on by tens and ones.
Then, fill in each blank.

**1**

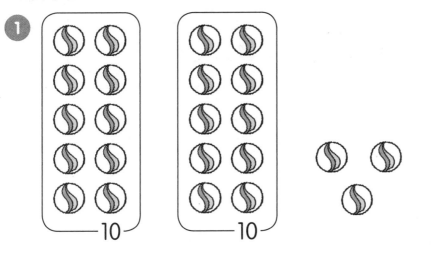

10, …, 20, _____, _____, _____

**2**

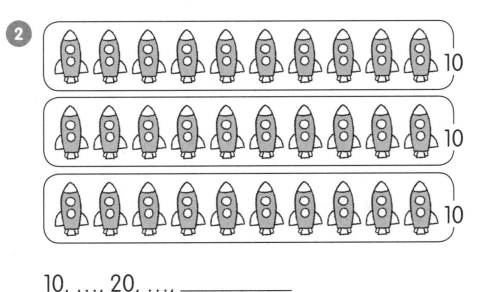

10, …, 20, …, _____

# Circle groups of 10.
# Then, count on and write each number.

**Example**

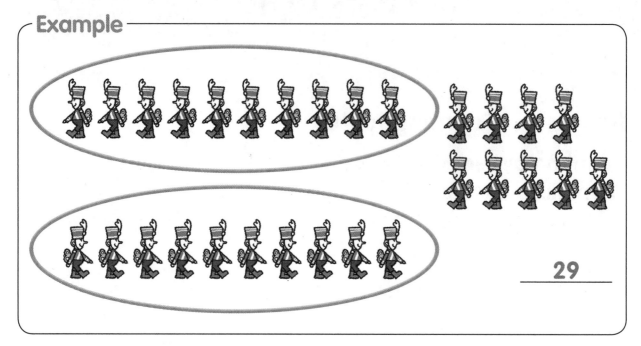

29

**3**

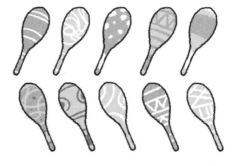

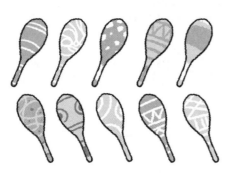

_____

**4**

_____

**5**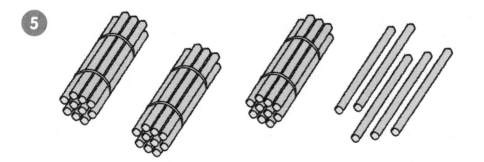

_____

**6**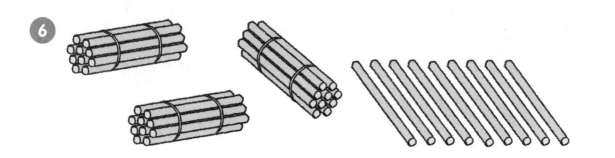

_____

# Count on by tens and ones.
# Then, write each number and word.

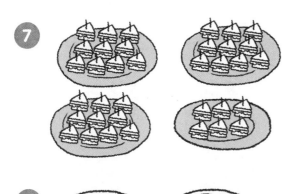

7

8

9

10

| Number | Word |
|---|---|
|  |  |
|  |  |
|  |  |
|  |  |

BLANK

# Extra Practice and Homework
## Numbers to 40

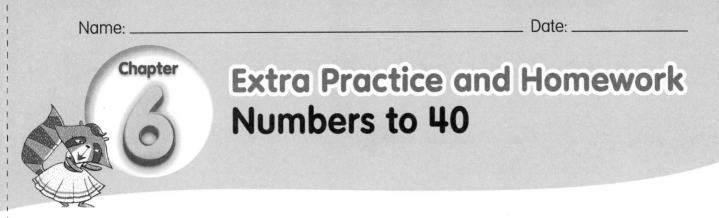

## Activity 2   Place Value

**Count on by tens and ones.**
**Then, fill in each blank.**

**1**

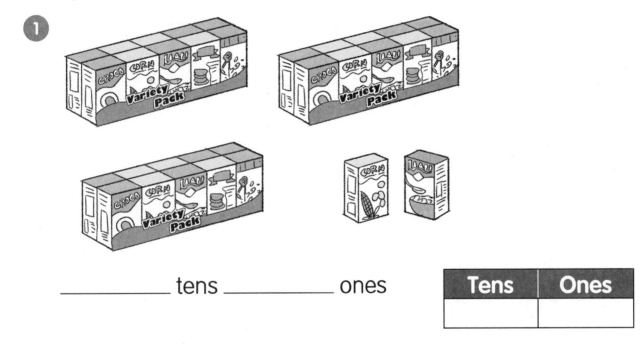

_____ tens _____ ones

| Tens | Ones |
|------|------|
|      |      |

**Look at each place-value chart.**
**Does the number of 🟦 and 🔹 match the number below them?**
**Write "Yes" or "No" in the blank.**

**2**

| Tens | Ones |
|------|------|
| 2    | 2    |

_____

**3**

| Tens | Ones |
|------|------|
| 3    | 8    |

_____

# Fill in each blank.

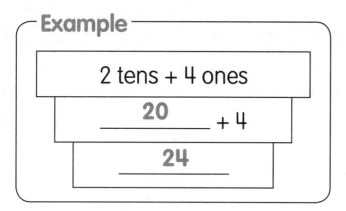

2 tens + 4 ones

__20__ + 4

__24__

**4**

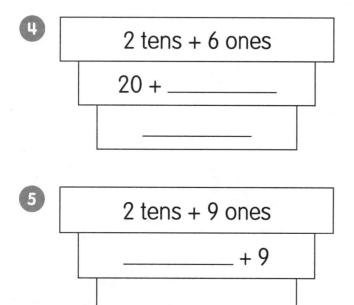

2 tens + 6 ones

20 + _____

_____

**5**

2 tens + 9 ones

_____ + 9

_____

**6**

| 3 tens + 5 ones |

30 + _____

_____

**7**

| 3 tens + 7 ones |

_____ + _____

_____

**8**

| 3 tens + 9 ones |

_____ + _____

_____

# Fill in each blank.
# Then, draw each missing picture.

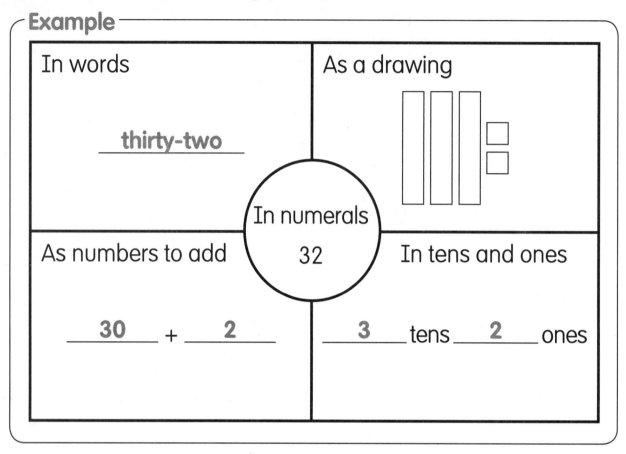

| In words | As a drawing |
|---|---|
| thirty-two | |

In numerals
32

| As numbers to add | In tens and ones |
|---|---|
| 30 + 2 | 3 tens 2 ones |

**9**

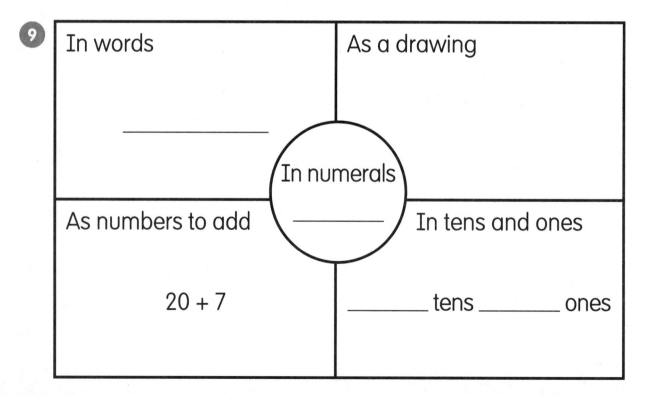

| In words | As a drawing |
|---|---|
| _____ | |

In numerals
_____

| As numbers to add | In tens and ones |
|---|---|
| 20 + 7 | _____ tens _____ ones |

**10**

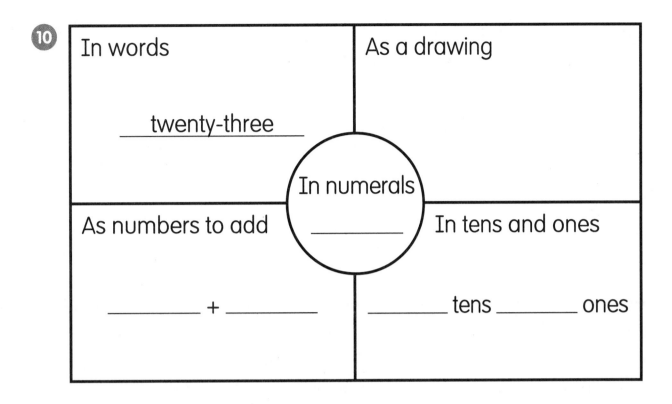

In words

_____twenty-three_____

As a drawing

In numerals

_____

As numbers to add

_____ + _____

In tens and ones

_____ tens _____ ones

**11**

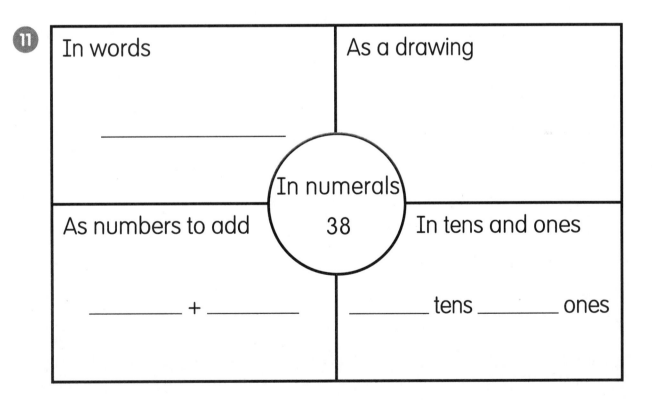

In words

_____

As a drawing

In numerals

38

As numbers to add

_____ + _____

In tens and ones

_____ tens _____ ones

BLANK

**Chapter 6**

## Extra Practice and Homework
## Numbers to 40

### Activity 3   Comparing, Ordering, and Number Patterns

**Count the objects in each group.**
**Then, fill in each blank.**

**1  a**

| Group A | Group B |
|---|---|

_____                    _____

**b**  There are fewer balls in Group _____ than in

Group _____.

**c**  There are more balls in Group _____ than in

Group _____.

**2** **a**

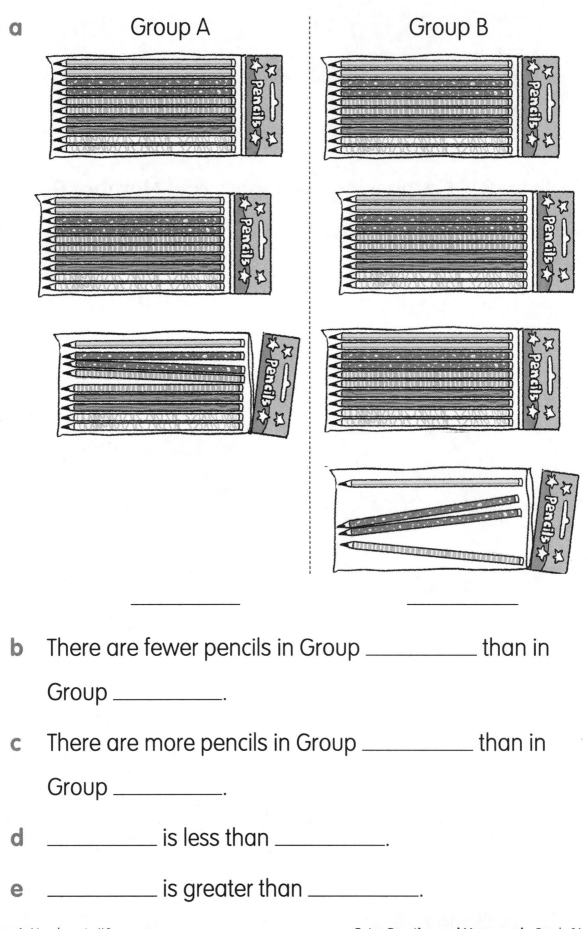

Group A                    Group B

_____          _____

**b** There are fewer pencils in Group _____ than in

Group _____.

**c** There are more pencils in Group _____ than in

Group _____.

**d** _____ is less than _____.

**e** _____ is greater than _____.

**Fill in each blank.**
**Use the counting tape to help you.**

| 25 | 26 | 27 | 28 | 29 | 30 | 31 | 32 | 33 | 34 | 35 | 36 | 37 | 38 |
|----|----|----|----|----|----|----|----|----|----|----|----|----|----|

**3** _____ is 3 less than 38.

**4** 2 less than 34 is _____.

**Compare each pair of numbers on the left.**
**Circle the correct answer.**
**Then, fill in each blank with "<," ">," or "=."**

**5** 34 | is less than / is greater than / is equal to | 34.          34 ◯ 34

**6** 40 | is less than / is greater than / is equal to | 33.          40 ◯ 33

**7** 36 | is less than / is greater than / is equal to | 39.          36 ◯ 39

# Order the numbers from least to greatest.

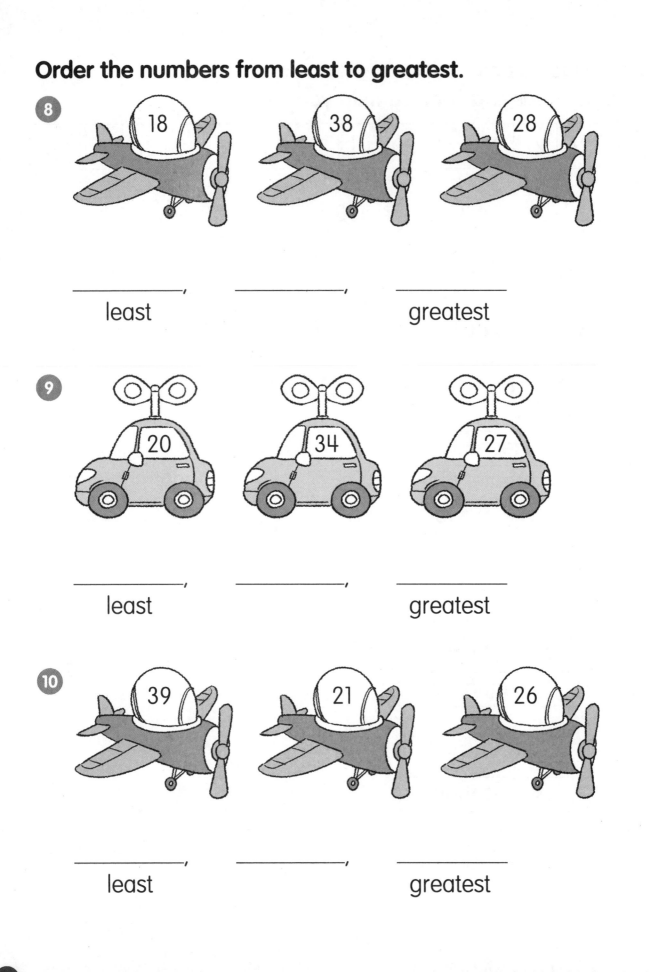

8

18    38    28

_____ , _____ , _____
least                          greatest

9

20    34    27

_____ , _____ , _____
least                          greatest

10

39    21    26

_____ , _____ , _____
least                          greatest

## Order the numbers from greatest to least.

**11** 23   32   33

_____, _____, _____
greatest        least

**12** 40   35   36

_____, _____, _____
greatest        least

**13** 24   37   29

_____, _____, _____
greatest        least

# Write the missing numbers in each number pattern.

14

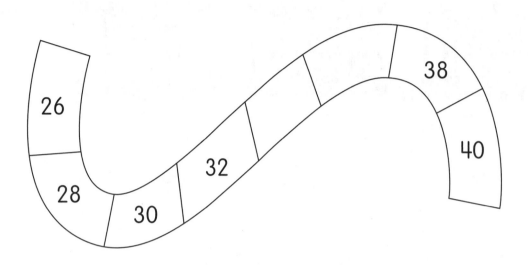

15

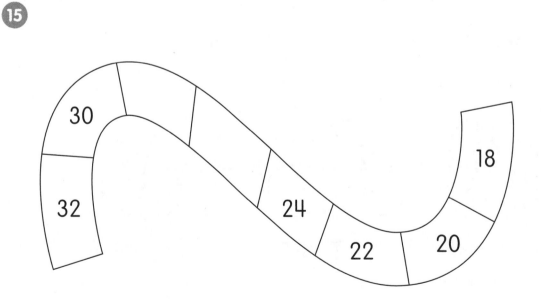

**Extra Practice and Homework** Grade 1A

**Mathematical Habit 2** Use mathematical reasoning

Look at the problem, and then the table.
The steps in the table to work out the problem are mixed up.
Number them correctly.

| Problem: |
|---|
| Order the numbers from least to greatest. |

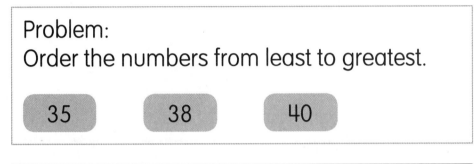

| The steps: | |
|---|---|
| | The greatest number is 40. |
| | So, 38 is greater than 35. |
| | Now, compare the ones in 35 and 38. |
| | Compare the tens. |
| | 35,              38,              40 <br> least                              greatest |
| | 8 ones are greater than 5 ones. |
| | 4 tens are greater than 3 tens. |

**1** | **Mathematical Habit** **1** **Persevere in solving problems**

Lydia covers part of her bracelet.
She asks Claire to guess how many beads are covered.
Lydia gives the clue that there are 36 beads in all.
How many beads are covered?

_____ beads are covered.

**2** **Mathematical Habit 1** **Persevere in solving problems**

Make a pattern that has the numbers below in it.

| 20 | 40 |

Pattern

**3** | Mathematical Habit **1** | **Persevere in solving problems**

Ava puts a ball with a number X into the machine.
A new ball numbered Y comes out from the machine.

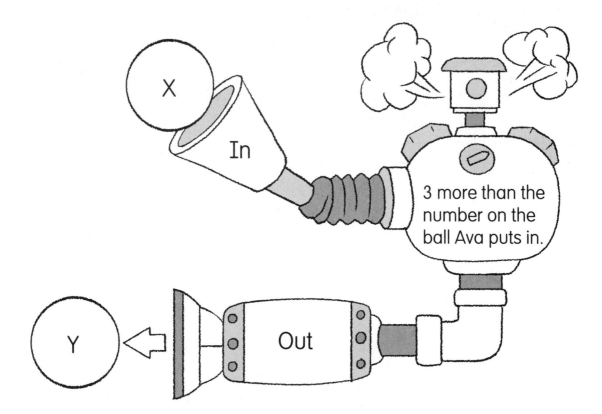

3 more than the number on the ball Ava puts in.

Y is less than 40, but greater than 31.
List 3 possible answers for X and Y.

# SCHOOL-to-HOME CONNECTIONS

## Chapter 7
## Calendar and Time

## Dear Family,

In this chapter, your child will learn to read a calendar and to tell time. Skills your child will practice include:

- reading a calendar
- knowing the seasons of the year
- reading and telling time to the hour and half hour
- relating time to daily activities

### Math Practice

At the end of this chapter, you may want to carry out these activities with your child. These activities will help to strengthen your child's understanding of how to read a calendar and how to tell time.

### Activity 1

- Use a paper calendar or go online to print a free calendar.
- Help your child make a list of family members' and friends' birthdays.
- Ask your child to mark their birthdays on the calendar.

### Activity 2

- Use a calendar to talk about the seasons of spring, summer, autumn, and winter. Discuss how the seasons where you live are the same and different from the seasons where others live.

### Activity 3

- Visit a library and read books about the seasons, such as *Red Sings from Treetops, A Year in Colors* by Joyce Sidman; *Green Eyes* by Abe Birnbaum; and *The Reasons for Seasons* by Gail Gibbons.

### Activity 4

- Ask your child to imagine a perfect day when he or she can do the things he or she likes. Have your child use the words "o'clock" and "half past" to talk about the things he or she would like to do at different times of the day.

### Math Talk

Examine a paper calendar or go online to print a free calendar. Discuss how the **days** are organized into **weeks**, weeks into **months**, and months into a **year**. Point to different dates on the calendar and ask your child to read the dates aloud.

Discuss the hands on a clock, and how we use the **hour hand** to read hours and the **minute hand** to read minutes. Talk about which times daily activities usually occur, such as waking up at **half past** six in the morning to get ready for school.

**BLANK**

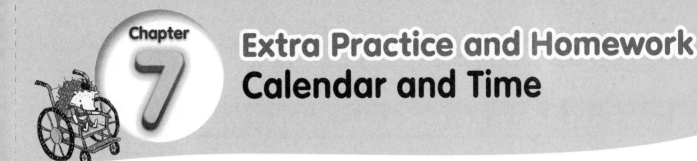

**Chapter 7**

# Extra Practice and Homework
## Calendar and Time

## Activity 1   Using a Calendar

**Fill in the blank.**

1  How many days are there in one week? _____

**Write the days of the week.**

Every week begins on a Sunday.

2  The first day is _____

3  The third day is _____

4  The fifth day is _____

5  The last day is _____

**Answer the question.**

6  Which is the day of the week you like best? _____

## Use the calendar to help you fill in each blank.

| JUNE 2018 | | | | | | |
|---|---|---|---|---|---|---|
| Sunday | Monday | Tuesday | Wednesday | Thursday | Friday | Saturday |
| | | | | | 1 | 2 |
| 3 | 4 | 5 | 6 | 7 | 8 | 9 |
| 10 | 11 | 12 | 13 | 14 | 15 | 16 |
| 17 | 18 | 19 | 20 | 21 | 22 | 23 |
| 24 | 25 | 26 | 27 | 28 | 29 | 30 |

**7** The name of the month is _____.

**8** There are _____ days in this month.

**9** _____ is the day between Wednesday and Friday.

**10** The date of the second Monday is _____

**11** The day of the week just after June 22, 2018

is _____.

**Look at the table.**
**Then, answer each question.**

| January | February | March |
|---------|----------|-----------|
| April | May | June |
| July | August | September |
| October | November | December |

**12** What is the month now?
Write it in the blank. _____

**13** Circle your birthday month in the table.

**14** Color the eighth month of the year green.

**15** Color the month with only 28 or 29 days blue.

**16** Color the months with only 30 days red.

# Match each picture to the correct season.

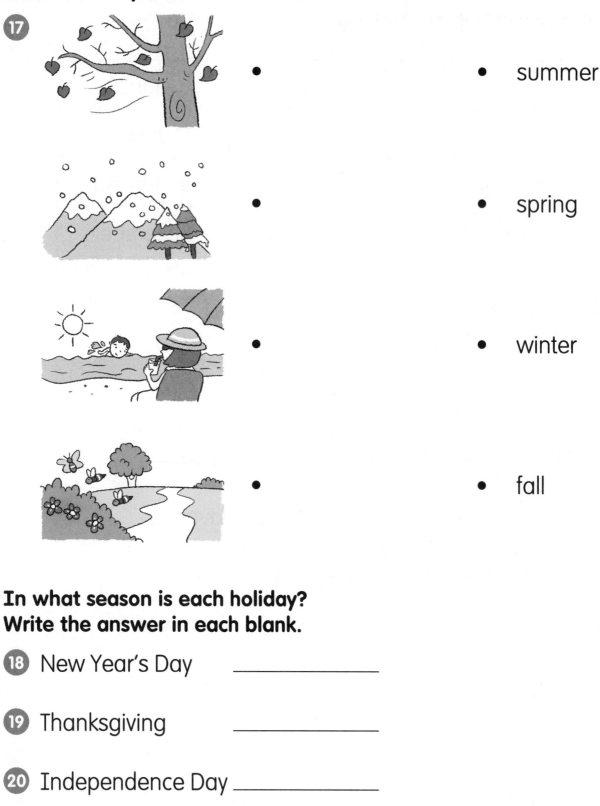

**17**

- • • summer

- • • spring

- • • winter

- • • fall

# In what season is each holiday?
# Write the answer in each blank.

**18** New Year's Day _____

**19** Thanksgiving _____

**20** Independence Day _____

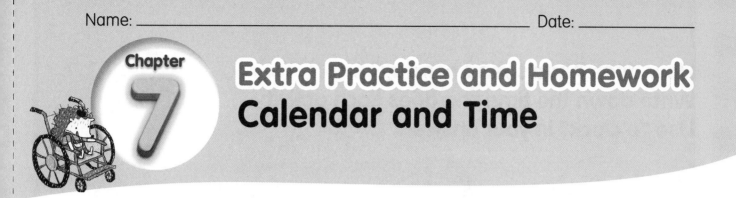

# Extra Practice and Homework
## Calendar and Time

## Activity 2   Telling Time to the Hour

**Match each clock to the correct time.**

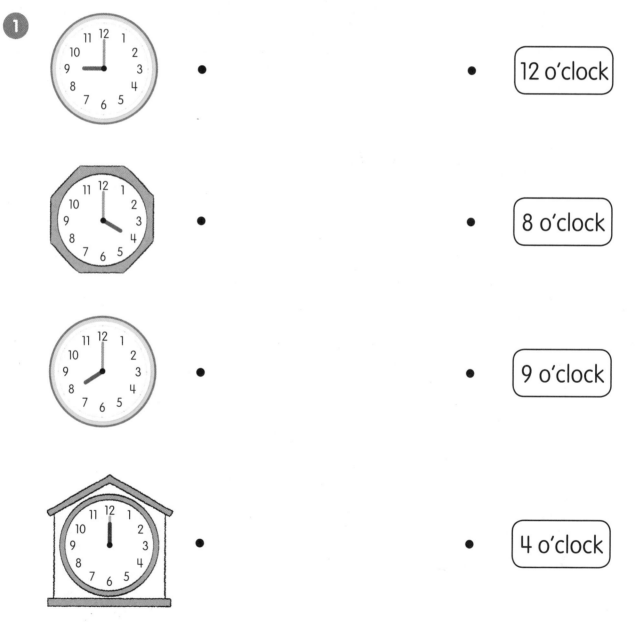

1

12 o'clock

8 o'clock

9 o'clock

4 o'clock

**How does Anna spend her day?**
**Write down the time she does each activity.**
**Use "o'clock" in your answer.**

Anna brushes her teeth at _____.

Anna's Math class starts at _____.

**4**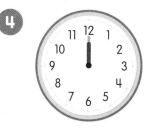

Anna has lunch at _____.

**5**

Anna plays with her friends at _____.

**6**

Anna practices playing the piano at _____.

**7**

Anna has her dinner at _____.

**8**

Anna does her homework at _____.

**9**

Anna goes to bed at _____.

# Look at each time on the left.
# Color the clock face that shows the correct time.

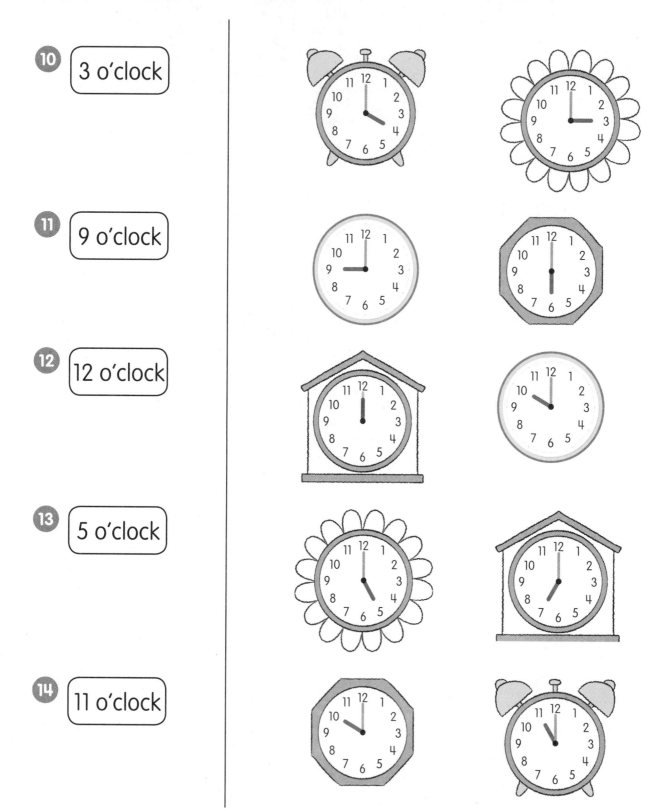

**10** 3 o'clock

**11** 9 o'clock

**12** 12 o'clock

**13** 5 o'clock

**14** 11 o'clock

# Match each clock to the correct time.

**15**

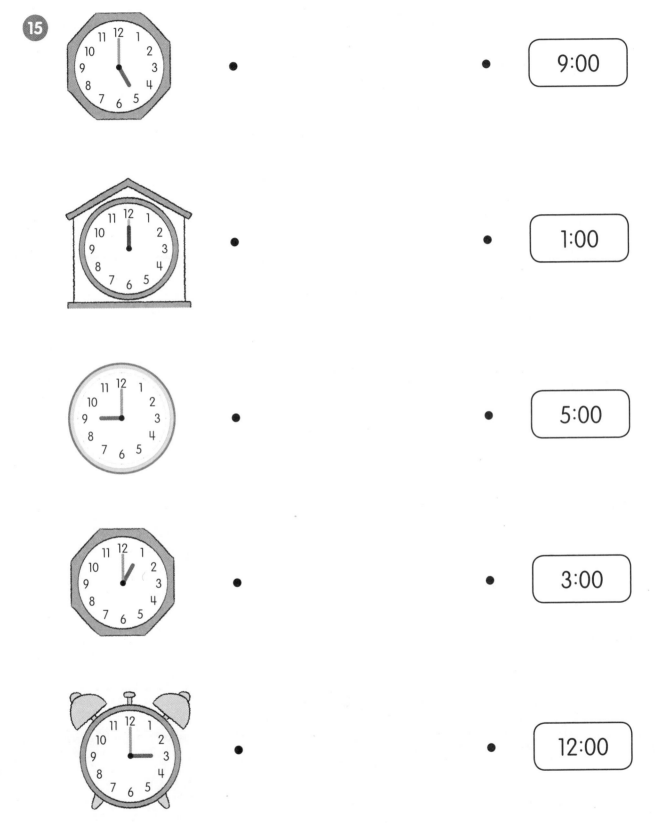

9:00

1:00

5:00

3:00

12:00

# Write each time in two ways.

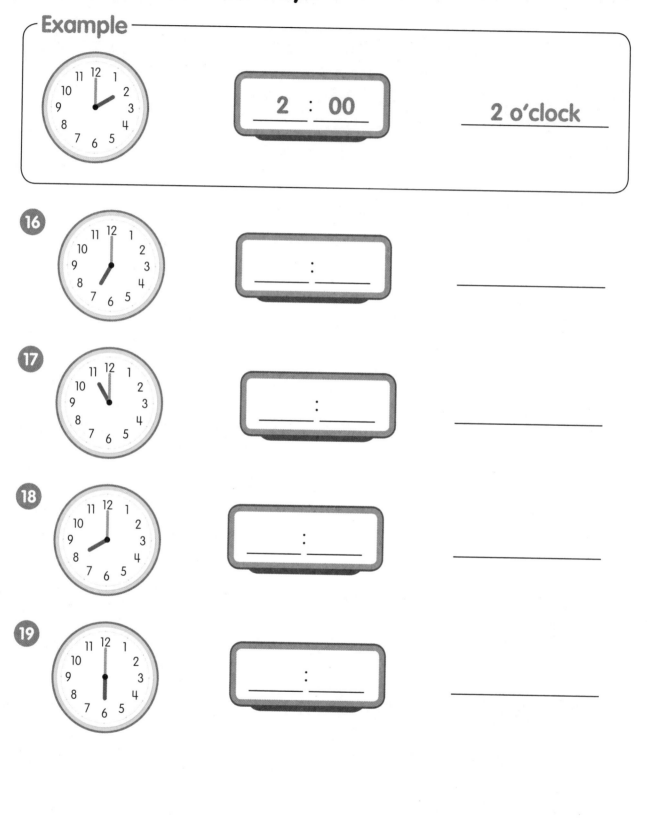

**Example**

2 : 00          2 o'clock

**16**          : _____          _____

**17**          : _____          _____

**18**          : _____          _____

**19**          : _____          _____

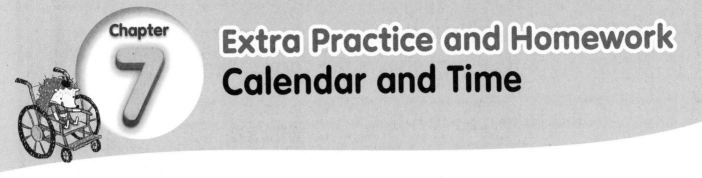

## Extra Practice and Homework
## Calendar and Time

**Chapter 7**

## Activity 3  Telling Time to the Half Hour

Match each clock to the correct time.

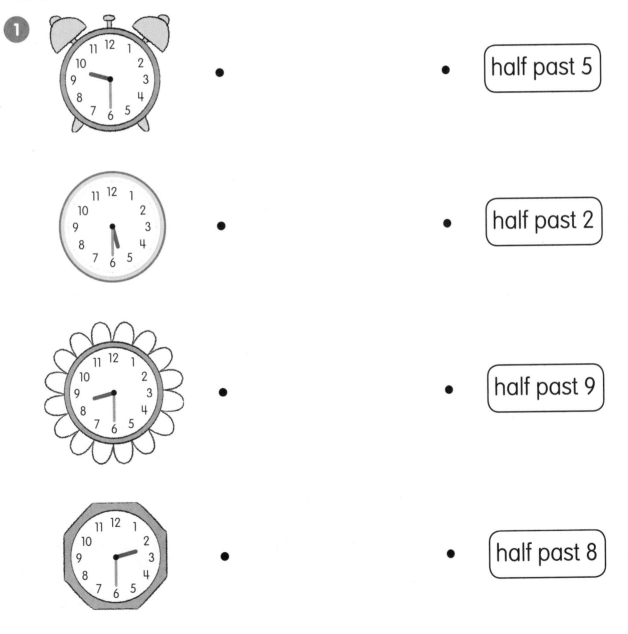

1

•          •  half past 5

•          •  half past 2

•          •  half past 9

•          •  half past 8

# Look at each time on the left.
## Color the clock face that shows the correct time.

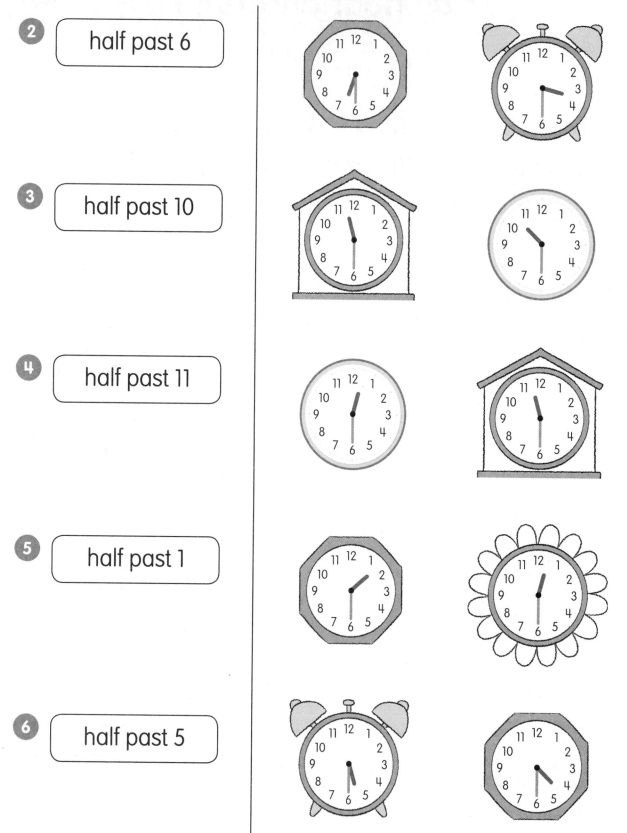

**2** half past 6

**3** half past 10

**4** half past 11

**5** half past 1

**6** half past 5

**The Jones family goes to the zoo on Sunday.**
**Write down the time they do each activity.**

**7**

They visit the bird and butterfly area at _____.

**8**

They look at the bears at _____.

**How do Pedro and his friends spend their Sunday?**
**Write down the time each child does each activity.**

**9**

Pedro goes to the bowling alley with his Dad at _____ o'clock.

**10**

John walks his cat at half past _____.

**11**

José cycles with his Dad at _____.

**12**

At _____, Aubrey enjoys lunch with her mother.

# Match each clock to the correct time.

12:30

11:30

4:30

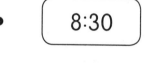
8:30

6:30

# Write each time in two ways.

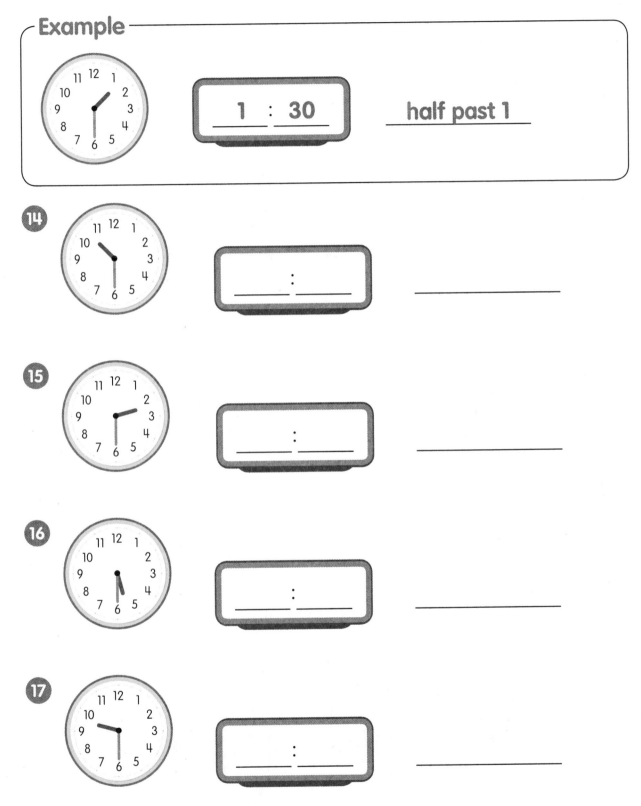

**Example**

1 : 30    half past 1

14

___ : ___    _____

15

___ : ___    _____

16

___ : ___    _____

17

___ : ___    _____

## What time is it now?
## Draw the missing hand on each clock.

**18** | half past 8

**19** | half past 12

**20** | 9:00

**21** | 1:30

**22** | 6:30

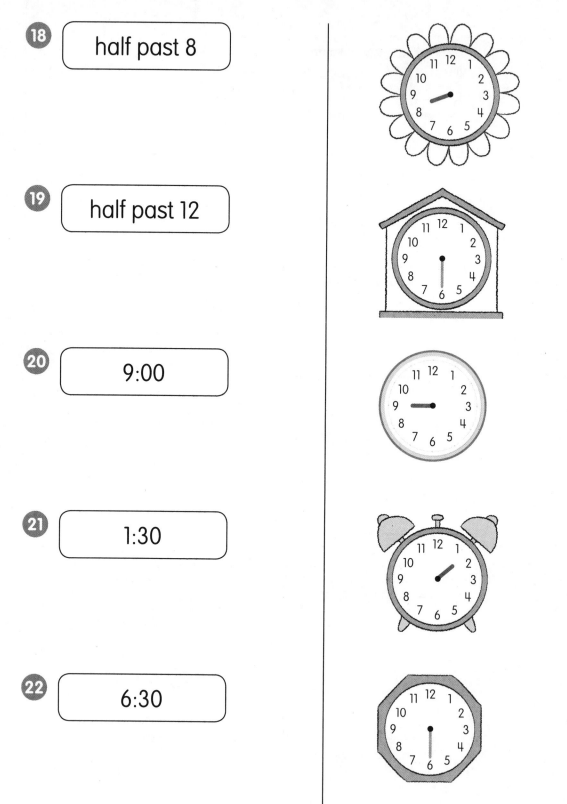

Name: _____ Date: _____

**1** **Mathematical Habit 6** **Use precise mathematical language**

Look at each clock.
Write about an activity you do at that time.
Use "o'clock" or "half past" in your sentence.

What I do in the morning...

_____

_____

What I do in the afternoon...

_____

_____

What I do at night ...

_____

_____

2 **Mathematical Habit** 6 **Use precise mathematical language**

Name the season you like best.
Write or draw to show why.

3 **Mathematical Habit** 6 **Use precise mathematical language**

Name the time of the day you like best.
Write this time to the hour or half hour.
Write or draw to show why.

**1** Mathematical Habit **2** Use mathematical reasoning

Peyton and her mother bake some muffins on Sunday.
Each picture shows the time they do an activity.
Number the pictures to show the correct order.

_____

_____

_____

_____ 1

**2** **Mathematical Habit 8** **Look for patterns**

Kaylee's hamsters chew off part of her calendar.

| September | | | | | | |
|---|---|---|---|---|---|---|
| Sun. | Mon. | Tue. | Wed. | Thu. | Fri. | Sat. |
| | | 1 | 2 | 3 | 4 | 5 |
| 6 | 7 | 8 | 9 | 10 | 11 | |
| 13 | 14 | 15 | 16 | | | |
| 20 | 21 | 22 | | | | |
| 27 | 28 | | | | | |

Look at the part of the calendar left.
Fill in each blank.

a    What is the date of the third Thursday? _____

b    What day of the week is September 25? _____

c    What day of the week does the next month

   begin on? _____

d    What date does the next month begin on?

   _____

e    How many Wednesdays are there in this month?

   _____